Clan
ROSS

The Ancient Clanna Siol Aindrea

COMPILED BY

Joseph R. Ross

HERITAGE BOOKS
2011

HERITAGE BOOKS
AN IMPRINT OF HERITAGE BOOKS, INC.

Books, CDs, and more—Worldwide

For our listing of thousands of titles see our website at
www.HeritageBooks.com

Published 2011 by
HERITAGE BOOKS, INC.
Publishing Division
100 Railroad Ave. #104
Westminster, Maryland 21157

Copyright © 2011 Joseph R. Ross

Other books by the author:
History Cape Negro and Blanche: Third Edition with Corrections

— Publisher's Notice —
Pages 128-130 have been removed from this reprint at the Author's request

All rights reserved. No part of this book may be reproduced or transmitted in any form or by any means, electronic or mechanical, including photocopying, recording or by any information storage and retrieval system without written permission from the author, except for the inclusion of brief quotations in a review.

International Standard Book Numbers
Paperbound: 978-0-7884-5230-7
Clothbound: 978-0-7884-8478-2

This book is in memory of my Father and Mother, Captain Willaim L. Ross and Anna Jane (Jenny) Smith Ross. My Mother helped me with my lessons and encouraged my interest in books, my Father taught me not to be afraid of hard work. Both principals have assisted in molding my life.

Contents

The Great Highland Clans.	Ch. 1.
Clan Ross - The Ancient Siol Aindrea.	Ch. 2.
The Highland Clearances.	Ch. 3.
The Crofters.	Ch. 4.
The Tartan.	Ch. 5.
The Claymore.	Ch. 6.
Highland Dancing, Music and Poetry.	Ch. 7.
Clan Ross Nova Scotia.	Ch. 8.
Acknowledgements.	

The McIan illustration of Ross as published (mid-19th century) in 'The Clans of the Scottish Highlands'

THE GREAT HIGHLAND CLANS

CHAPTER 1

The Clans

The Gaelic word Clan means children, and when considered it explains aptly the close relationship that once existed between the chief and his Clansmen. The word Clan being Gaelic it should rightly only apply to those of that heritage.

When the Celtic laws were in operation the bond between the Chief and Clansmen was very close. It was only when feudal rules and ideas were introduced in Scotland that a gulf gradually developed, and the attitude of the Chief being the landowner, and the Clansmen subservant tenants evolved.

This decline eventually led to the despotic behaviour of some Clan Chiefs, who had become anglicised landlords and overly class conscious. These Chiefs evicted their people from their ancestral lands, in a most cruel and ruthless manner. These evictions are usually refered to as the "Clearances of the Highlands," and took place whereby the cleared lands could be rented out as sheep walks, bringing more money to the Chief than what was obtained from his Clansmen. Clansmen were replaced by sheep.

Vast areas of Ross-shire today are empty of populace, and only the crumbling walls of hundreds of stone cottages in these large glens, attest to the cruel eviction of the Clansmen of Ross.

Under ancient Celtic rule and custom the land belonged to the Clan, not to a person. The Chief held a superiority of it but only in name of the Clan, as its father. The early Clan system was aristocratic but not feudal. The people were free and could speak as equals to their chief, as children to a father. This relationship ceased when the evictions began.

Most Clansmen did not resist to any great degree being evicted from their homes and lands, because they were accustomed to trusting and obeying the wishes of their

Chief. They however could not understand his actions in this matter, but nevertheless sadly complied.

Highland Clans such as the Ross's were Gaelic speakers, a rich, beautiful and sensitive language, which is one of the oldest in Europe, and still survives today in the Western Highlands of Scotland and some off shore Islands.

Nova Scotia has a number of communities where the Gaelic is still spoken, and also has the famous Gaelic Collage, at St. Ann's, Cape Breton, where the Gaelic language is taught and also Gaelic music, piping and highland dancing.

Scotland is divided in the center by the Grampian Mountains. The area north is the Highlands and the people were Gaelic speakers. The area south is the Lowlands and the people spoke English. The mountain division and speaking different languages produced two distinct people. Today some Lowland families claim to be Clans, which they are definately not, as they have no justifiable claim to the Gaelic word - Clan.

The Highlanders of old operated a cattle economy, thousands of small, black cattle were reared. Goats were also kept. Fishing and deer hunting were also carried out.

The word black-mail originates in Scotland's Southern Highlands. It's not quite as bad as it sounds. Some Clans said to the Lowland landowners, "pay us money and we will not steal your cattle" and will not let anyone else do it either. It was a form of primitive policing. Black-mail derives from Black for colour of cattle (present day shaggy cattle are 19th. century crossbreeds) and mail from a Scots word for rent.

Scots who migrated or were forcibly transported, to what is now Canada and United States, sometimes did spectularly well in the cattle business, and some of their descendents left their Clan mark on the map forever, as with the old Chisholm trail.

The Gaelic pattern of the shieling, when each Spring and summer the people took themselves from the lower glens to the upper glens and moors, the people living in makeshift huts and supervising the grazing cattle and goats, fattening them for sale, or the winter, and making butter and cheese.

The Ross Clansmen considered war a manly pursuit, and with only oatmeal to sustain them could march for miles and then fight a battle at the end of it. Their weapons were broadswords and claymores (big or great sword), bows and arrows, Lochaber axes, dirks (long dagger) and targe (a round shield) and, in later centuries muskets and pistols.

Led well, there has possibly been no finer infantry. They were uneasy in street fighting or facing cannon fire, but in a charge - as Neil Munro says - they would carry the very Gates of Hell even if the Devil himself stood in the portals.- Ferocious fighters.

Prince Charles Edward Stuart raised his standard in 1745,which ended at the last Highland battle at Culloden, this last battle is well documented in John Prebbles book on the subject and is recommended reading, following this battle the Hanoverian King of England, German George 1, the victor, banned the use of weapons, wearing of Tartan, playing the pipes and the Chiefs authority. The Clan system was broken up, and all that is left now are memories, modern Clan Societies, and thousands of Scots, or people of Scot descent, who have a pride in an ancestry that was staunch, courageous, colourful, war-like, cultured, vigorous, and full of zest.

The Highland Clans and Lowland Families

Anderson
Armstrong
Baird
Balmoral
Barclay
Brodie
Bruce
Buchanan
Cameron
Cameron of Lochiel
Cameron of Erracht
Campbell
Campbell of Breadalbane
Campbell of Cawdor
Chisholm
Clan Chattan
Clergy
Colquhoun
Cumming
Cumin
Comyne
Cunningham
Davidson
Douglas
Drummond
Duncan
Elliot
Erskine
Farquharson
Fergus(S)on
Fletcher
Forbes
Fraser of Lovat
Gordon
Gow
Graham
Grant
Gunn
Gunn of Kilernan
Hamilton
Hay
Henderson
Innes
Johnston
Keith
Kennedy
Kerr
Lamont
Leslie
Lindsay
Livingstone
Logan
MacAlister
MacAlpine
MacAndrew
MacArthur
MacAulay

ROSS

MacBain
MacCallum
MacColl
MacDonald
MacDonald of the Isles
MacDonald of Sleat
MacDonald of Clanranald
MacDonell of Glengarry
MacDonell of Keppoch
Macdougall
MacDuff
MacEwen
MacFarlane
Macfie
MacGillivray
MacGowen
MacGregor
MacInnes
MacIntyre
MacIver
MacKay
MacKendrick
MacKenzie
MacKinnon
MacIntosh
MacLachlan
Maclaine of Lochbuie
MacLaren
MacLean
MacLeod of MacLeod
MacLeod
MacMillan
MacNab
MacNaughton
MacNeil(1) of Bara
MacNicol
MacPherson

MacQuarrie of Ulva
MacQueen of Corybrough
MacRae
Malcolm
Matheson
Maxwell
Melville
Menzies
Montgomery
Morrison
Munro
Murray
Murray of Athol
Napier
Nicholson
Ogilvie
Oliphant
Ramsay
Rob Roy
Robertson
Rose
Ross
Scott
Shaw
Sinclair
Skene
Stewart
Stewart of Appin
Sutherland
Urquhart
Wallace

Bonnie Prince Charlie - 1745.

Of all the famous and historic personalities that have emerged from the history of the Scottish Highlands, that of Charles Edward Stuart, son of James, Pretender to the throne of Scotland, is perhaps the most colourful. Born in exile on the Continent, the Prince needed only the persuasion of Irish exiles like Sir Thomas Sheridan and Scots advisers like Murray of Broughton to tempt him to sail to Scotland and make a bold bid for the Scottish Crown.

He came in the summer of 1745 on a little ship, the *Doutelle,* after a skirmish in the Channel with an English warship during which the *Elizabeth,* a companion vessel, was hard hit and returned to harbour. MacDonald of Boisdale met him on the island of Eriskay where the Prince first landed.

'Go home,' advised the chief who was doubtful of the wisdom of the enterprise.

'I am come home, sir,' replied the young adventurer, and continued his voyage, to land with seven trusted followers at Moidart.

At first it seemed that MacDonald's advice had been wise. The clan chiefs received him with uncertainty, afraid to commit themselves to so uncertain a venture. Even Cameron of Lochiel held back, but in the end he came under the spell of the eager young man who had set his hopes on attaining success. Lochiel and his seven hundred clansmen accompanied Charles to Glen Finnan, where the Standard was raised.

From then on success seemed assured. The clans rallied, the Jacobite army began to grow in strength, until Lord George, Earl of Murray, the Prince's aide-de-camp, commanded a force of two thousand five hundred men and marched to the capital.

Sir John Cope, who was in command of the regular army, made a half-hearted attempt to intercept the rebels, then turned tail for Inverness. The road to Edinburgh was open, and in a few days Charles had entered the city, opposition having been easily overcome. The hearlds raised their trumpets. James VIII was proclaimed king at the Mercat Cross.

Cope returned and approached Edinburgh from the east. With the army at the gates Charles gathered his men and prepared to join battle. After a brilliant charge Cope's men were put to flight by the Highlanders, and he himself escaped to carry the news of his own sorry rout to Berwick.

Had Charles shown wisdom and followed up his first successes by marching straightway into England, history might have read differently today, But he tarried in the city to celebrate his good fortune. From then on disaster followed on the heels of defeat, until the Jacobite army that had marched so proudly across the border, almost to the walls of London, was in the end destroyed and disbanded in Culloden Moor.

Charles retreated to the island of North Uist where he had counted on boarding a ship to France. But the island was well-nigh overrun with soldiers and he himself carried a price of £30,000 pounds on his head.

It is to the credit of the islanders that no-one sought to reveal his presence. Eventually a lady, Flora MacDonald, came to his rescue. She obtained a permit to land in Skye with her maid 'Betty Burke.' The Prince disguised himself in woman's clothes, assumed the name and identity of Flora's maid, and after a perilous journey reached the romantic misty isle.

Alas, it was only to discover that Skye, like North Uist, was a place of danger. He reached the mainland and concealed himself in a cave with seven known robbers as companions. From thence he made his way over the mountains to Ben Aldur. This time his hiding-place was 'Cluny's Cage,' a rude hut built of sticks hidden in the trees on the mountain-side, where Cluny himself and Cameron of Lochiel kept his whereabouts unknown for many days.

Not until September in the year 1746, five long months after Culloden, did he manage to make his way to a ship. He sailed from Scotland, never to return, and died an inglorious death in squalor in 1788.

With his departure came a time of sorrow and humiliation for the Highlands. The clan system was destroyed, rights and privileges taken away, and even the tartan which the clans loved so dearly was forbidden as a dress. But the memory of the Young Pretender who had come so near to wearing the Scottish crown, and who had endeared himself to rich and poor alike with his ready laugh and charm of manner, continued to live long after the last bitter defeat of a lost cause.

Prince Charles Edward Stuart

CLAN ROSS

THE ANCIENT CLANNA SIOL AINDREA

Acknowledgement - Following are excerpts of History of Clan Ross, by Alexander M. Ross. 1932. Scotland.

CHAPTER 2

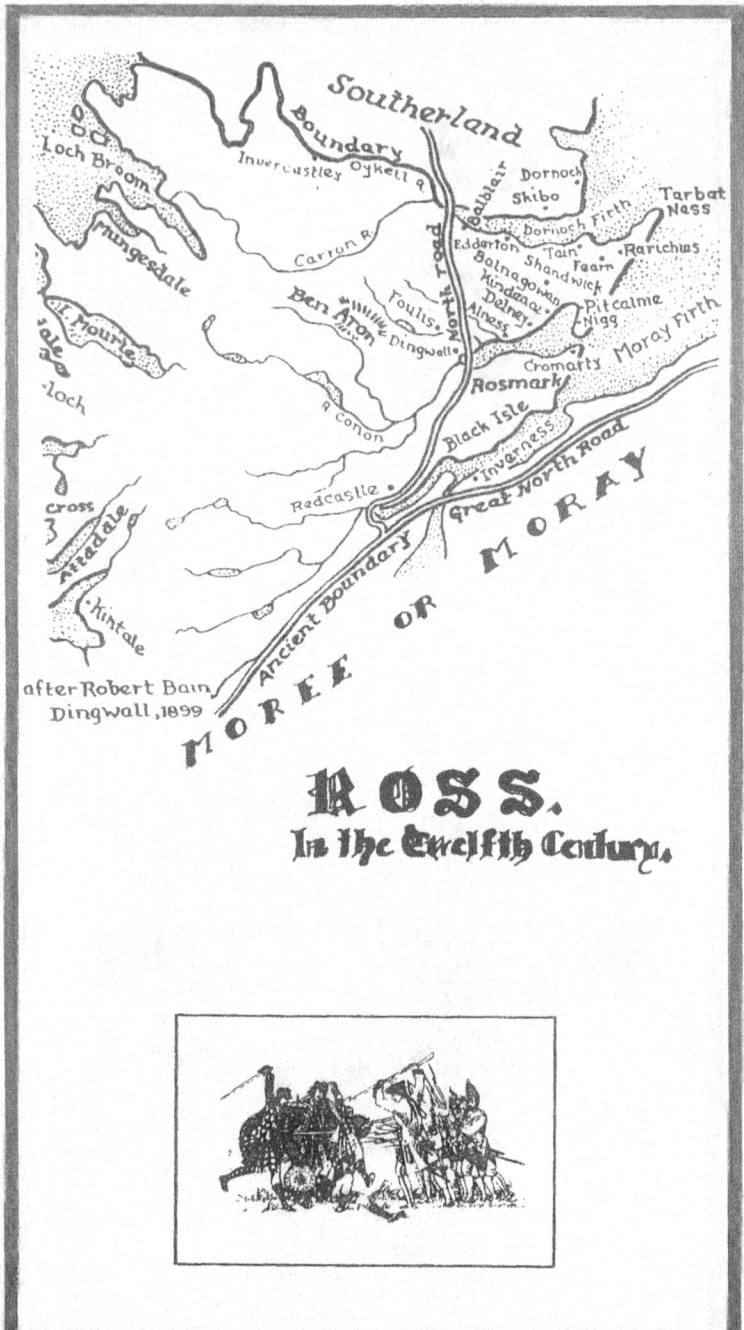

Contrary to the common belief, Ross-Shire is not named after the Rosses. Ross county, as Skene in "Highlanders of Scotland" writes, "is mentioned in the North Sagas along with the districts which were ruled by Mormaors or Jarls," but it is not the case, as Skene also observes, that it was only upon the downfall of the powerful race of Moray Mormaors that "the Chiefs of Ross first appear in history." Skene is right if by the Chiefs of Ross he means the Earls of that name, but there were no Earls who bore the surname Ross. The surname did not come into existence until after the death of the fifth Earl of Ross, when his brother, Hugh of Rarichies (son of Hugh, fourth Earl of Ross), the progenitor of the Rosses of Balnagown, took over the name of the County as his surname. Nisbet ("System of Heraldry") writes—"Hugh Ross of Rarichies, son of Hugh, Earl of Ross, who was killed in the battle of Halidon Hill, got from his father the lands of Rarichies, as also the lands of Easterallan from his brother Willaim, Earl of Ross, 1357; and these lands were confirmed by a charter of King David II."

On this point—the origin of the surname Ross—Sir Robert Gordon ("Earldom of Sutherland") says:—"From the second son of the Earl of Ross the lairds of Balnagowan are descended, and had by inheritance the lands of Rarieches and Coulleigh, where you may observe that the laird of Balnagowan's surname should not be Ross, seeing that there was never any Earl of Ross of that surname; but the Earls of Ross were first of the surname of Beolan, then they were Leslies, and last of all that earldom fell by inheritance to the Lords of the Isles, who resigned the same into King James the Third's hands in the year of God 1477. So I do think that the lairds of Balnagowan, perceiving the Earls of Ross decayed, and that earldom fallen into the Lord of the Isles hands, they called themselves Ross, thereby to testify their descent from the Earls of Ross."

But the fact of their descent from the Earls of Ross (from the first five) allows us to claim that the line goes back for several centuries anterior to the fourteenth. The first Earl of Ross (as referred to later in our sketch of the Earls) was Fearcher (Farquhar), son of the "Sagart" or priest who was a lay abbot of Applecross, who was the son of Gillianrias, a descendant of Beolan or Gilleon na h'Airde, the reputed ancestor of the Mackenzies, the Mathesons, the Gillanders, the Andrews and Macandrews, the Taggarts and Mactaggarts, the Mactears and Mactires, as well as (by descent from the Earls of Ross) the Rosses. Buchanan of Auchmar quotes an old account of the origin of the Rosses which derives them from the Norse, but of this there is no proof beyond the statement.

The Gaelic name of the Clan Ross is "Siol Aindrea," Clann Aindrea or Anrias. This, with other particulars, is referred to by Skene (in his "Highlanders of Scotland" already mentioned) as follows:—

"It is well known that the surname of Ross has always been rendered in Gaelic *clan Anrias* or *clan Gille Anrias*, and that they appear under the former of these appellations in all the early Acts of Parliament; there is also an unvarying tradition in the Highlands that on the death of Willaim, last Earl of Ross of this family, a certain Paul MacTire was for some time Chief of the clan, and this tradition is corroborated by the fact that there is a charter by this William, Earl of Ross, to this very Paul MacTire, in which he styles him his cousin. There appears, however, among the numerous clans contained in the MS. of 1450, one termed Clan Gilleanrias, which commences with Paul MacTire, so that there can be little doubt that this clan is the same with that of the Rosses, and in this MS. they are traced upwards in a direct line to a certain 'Gilleon na h'Airde' or Collin of Aird, who must have lived in the tenth century."

In an Act of Parliament, passed in 1587, the names of all the Highland Clans are specified, and among them Clan Anrias or the Rosses. By that year the Rosses were among the most numerous of the family names in Ross-Shire.

In the 1845 "Statistical Account," the following occurs under Tain—"Most of the landowners, and in truth most of the people, bore the name of Ross, or, to speak more correctly, almost everybody possessed two surnames, by one of which (in general a patronymic beginning with Mac.) he was universally known in conversation, though he deemed himself called upon to change it to Ross, whenever he acquired any status in society, or became able to write his name. . . . When the by-names of those who had risen in society had been forgotten, it became absolutely necessary to invent others to distinguish the multitudes of Rosses. We Quote this as evidence of the growth of the Clan as founded by Hugh of Rarichies in the fourteenth century.

In a list of the numbers of Highland Clans that were to be raised for King James, in 1704, the Rosses of Balnagown are credited with 300.

In the 1715 (Jacobite) Rebellion the Rosses—gave 700 men to His Majesty's cause, taking part with the Argyle men, Lord Sutherland's, Lord Lovat's Frasers, the Grants, the Roses, and the Forbes Clan. The Mackenzies with the Macdonalds, Macleods, Camerons, Chisholms, Mackintoshs, taking the side of the "rebels."

As anti-Jacobites, the Rosses played a gallant part in the many encounters in the north with the Jacobite Clans, but probably no episode in which they figured has more interest to-day than the part which two of the Clan played in collecting the rents of the forfeited Seaforth estates when the redoubtable Murchison, factor for

Seaforth,—a soldier as well as estate chamberlain—got the rents sent to his exiled Chief. We refer in detail to this in our record of the Rosses of Easter Fearn.

Some seventy years before the Jacobite Risings—to give an indication of the standing of the Rosses centuries ago—an Alexander Ross was chaplain in ordinary to King Charles II. In 1642 he published "Mel Heliconium," or "Poetical Honey gathered out of the Weeds of Parnassus." It was to this Ross that Samuel Butler in his "Hudibras" refers in the couplet.

> There was an ancient sage philosopher,
> Who had read Alexander Ross over!

He must, indeed, have been of tough philosophic fibre, but, whatever his accomplishments, it is of interest to the Rosses that a Clansman was so long ago the friend of Royalty and that he has achieved immortality— even if it be in the pages of Butler's classic satire.

Like all other Highland Clans, the Rosses have several septs and dependants. The full list, as commonly allowed, is as follows—Anderson, Andrew, Dingwall, Gillanders, Macandrew, Macculloch, Maclulich, Mactaggart, Mactear, Mactier, Mactire, Taggart, Vass, and Wass. Of these, the Dingwalls, the Macculllochs. and the Vasses, were at times associated with other clans, but chiefly with the Munros, taking part with them in several of their feuds in olden times. The Vasses, or Wasses, took a considerable share in the Ross fightings. At Aldicharrish, in 1487, when the forces under Alexander Ross of Balnagown, Chief of the Rosses, were severly defeated by the combined forces of the Sutherlands and MacKays, many of the name of Vass (given as Waus) were slain, In the same conflict, Angus Macculloch of Tarrell, "one of the gentlemen of Ross of Balnagowan", was also among the slain. The Tarrell Macculllochs first appear in record about the year 1368. In 1458, John of Ile, Earl of Ross, and Sheriff of Inverness, addressed to John Macculloch, bailie of the girth of Sanct Duthowis, a letter requiring him to protect the privileges of Innernys in that quarter. In 1512, King James IV granted anew to William Macculloch of Pladdis the lands of Scardy, Pladdis, Petnely, Pettogarty, Balmoduthy (apparently Bailedhuich or Tain), and Ballecarew, with the office of Bailie of the immunity of Tane, in the earldom of Ross and sheriffdom of Innernys which William had resigned, reserving to the King the escheats of the bailie courts, for the usual services and the yearly payment of five marks to a perpetual chaplain in the cathedral church of Ross. The Maccullochs' holdings in the province of Ross appear to have been very considerable, for we find them in possession of the lands of Piltoun, Mulderg, Bellnagore, Easter Drumm, etc. A charter, dated 1649, by Walter Ross of Bellamuckie, conveys to Andrew Macculloch, Provost of Tain, the two last named estates. In 1674 the Lyon King of Arms matriculates the coat armour of Sir Hugh Macculloch as "being descended of the family of Cadboll in Rosse."

The Dingwalls, Gillanders, Macandrews, and Mactaggarts had association with the Rosses at various dates, and the MacTire connections have been already referred to. The Gillanders have never been a numerous Clan, but they have had a family history as respectable as it is ancient. In a 1450 genealogical MS. of the Mathesons it is stated that the Ross portions of North Argyll were in the hands of several Ross-shire Clans, the Gillanders being mentioned among the Mathesons and the Mackenzies. They are referred to by a later chronicler—who quotes the same MS.—as "Rosses."

THE EARLS OF ROSS

The title of Ross was enjoyed by the progenitors of Clan Ross well known as early as the reign of King Malcolm IV., who succeeded to the Crown of Scotland in 1163. The first who bore the title was Malcolm. He was of the Celtic family of O'Bealan or Builton.

Earl Farquhar flourished in the reign of King Alexander II., who succeeded William the Lion. About this time a rebellion broke out in the Province of Ross and Moray, and Farquhar rendered signal service in quelling it. In recognition of his efforts he was created Earl of Ross, with lordship rights over lands in Ross, Skye, the Lewis, Moray, as well as subsequently in Galloway, where Earl Farquhar again took King Alexander out of difficulties.

Chivalrous, a man of restless activity— physically powerful and of superb courage— he was a heroic figure in his time. He was high in the Royal counsels, and was one of the Commission of Scottish noblemen who went to Rome in 1244 to inform the pope that Scotland and England had concluded a treaty of peace. It was at this time, while as a guest of the English King, that he took part in one of those knightly combats which were a favourite pastime with Royalty. Challenged by a French courtier, who was renowned for his strength and skill with sword and lance, Earl Farquhar agreed to show what a Ross-shire Highlander could do in that line. He won handsomely in the encounter. He had vowed that if he survived the combat he would found a religious house in Ross-shire. In the year 1230, he founded the Abbey of Ferne (Fearn) in the Parish of Edderton. The Abbey, not long after its foundation, was removed to a site several miles distant, and in subsequent years it was known as the "Abbacia de Nova Farina." In 1251 the Earl died and was buried within the later Fearn Abbey, and a stone effigy marks the spot where he lies.

Farquhar was succeeded by his son William, who made a great figure in the reign of Alexander III. He was one of the Scottish nobles who became bound not to conclude a peace with England without the consent of the Prince and Nobles of Wales. He confirmed his father's donations to the Abbacy of Ferne in the year 1258. Afterwards, with several others of the Scottish nobility, he bound and obliged himself to maintain and defend Princess Margaret's title to the Crown of Scotland in the event of Alexander III. dying without male issue. He obtained a grant of the Isle of Skye and the Lewis from Alexander III. He died in 1274 at Earles Allane. He was married to Jean, daughter of William Comyn, Earl of Buchan.

William was succeeded by his son William, Fourth Earl of Ross, who lived in stirring times, consequent on the death of the Maid of Norway. In 1283 he was one of the nobles who acknowledged the Maid of Norway as heir of the Crown. He sided alternately with the English and Scottish parties, as did several others of the Scottish nobles, "preferring that which concerned their own interests" to that of their country. At Berwick, in 1291, the Earl did homage to Edward I. as overlord. Five years later, the Scottish Army, under the Earls of Ross.

Menteith and Athole, made an incursion into England, devastating the country. They succeeded in occupying the Castle of Dunbar, which did not, however, continue long in their possession. The Scots were ultimately routed with a loss of 10,000 men besides a number of prisoners. The latter included the Earl of Ross, who was sent to the Tower of London, where he was condemned to live on sixpence per day. He was kept in close confinement for three years, and after the expiry of that period, an order for his escort and guard, with explicit directions for the journey to Scotland, was issued.

While her husband was in the Tower, the Countess of Ross (a partisan of the English) obtained a safe conduct to London to see the Earl, and was allowed by Edward £100 for her travelling expenses.

In 1305 he was appointed Warden beyond the Spey. No doubt it was in the full consciousness of his great authority as such, or perhaps it was on account of the craven dread he had of Edward, that this Earl committed one of the meanest of the many mean acts which history records. It will be recalled that on the advance of the English into Scotland, Bruce's Queen, not judging the Castle of Kildrummie, where she had taken shelter, strong enough to protect her, had resolved to betake herself to Sanctuary where even felons and murderers were safe under the powerful guardianship of the Church. With her young step-daughter, Marjory, the anxious Queen set out for St. Duthac, Tain, accompanied by an armed escort; but, unhappily, for the Earl of Ross, now on the side of the English, violated the Sanctuary by seizing the fugitives and delivering them into the hands of Edward.

After being kept in guard for several years the distinguished prisoners were set at liberty.

The Earl of Ross and the "men beyond the mountains" were bitterly opposed to Bruce, and the latter could scarcely forget the Earl's conduct when fortune smiled upon him. Accordingly, in 1307, he invaded Ross and Sutherland, and the inhabitants of these regions were so terrified that they petitioned the English King for assistance, The required aid did not come, however, and Bruce took signal vengeance upon the Earl, and ravaged his lands, which made him glad to sue for pardon and make a truce. They met at Auldearn, and here the Earl swore fealty—this reconciliation being cemented by the marriage of that Earl's son, Hugh, with the Princess Maud, sister of the King. The Earl was also infefted into the lands of Dingwall and Ferncrosky (Croick).

In 1312, Earl William appended his seal to the agreement between the Kings of Scotland and Norway. He led the men of Ross at the Battle of Bannockburn, and was one of those who addressed the famous letter of the Independence of Scotland. The "Kalendar of Fearn" bears that he died at Delny on the 28th. of January,1322.

His wife, Euphemia, sympathised with the English and during her husband's imprisonment in the Tower of London, her comfort was not forgotten, Edward having granted her ample maintenance from her husband's lands.

William was succeeded by his son Hugh, as Fifth Earl of Ross. By various Charters granted by Robert I., this Earl received the lands of Skye, Strathglass, Strathconon, etc. He was in command of the Reserve which attacked the wing under Baliol at the Battle of Halidon Hill, near Berwick, and was slain in 1333. It is of interest to mention that on his body was found the shirt of St. Duthac, which was supposed to possess miraculous powers, It is only fair to the English to state that the shirt was returned to the Sanctuary at Tain.

Hugh was married twice—first to Lady Maud Bruce, sister to the King, and (2) to Margaret, daughter of Sir David Graham of Old Montrose. By the first union he had two sons and a daughter, and by his second wife, Hugh of Rarichies, who afterwards became the progenitor of the Rosses of Balnagown, while a daughter, Euphemia, became the Queen of Robert II.

William, eldest son of Hugh, Fifth Earl, by his first wife, Lady Maud Bruce, became the Sixth Earl. He was resident in Norway when his father died, and did not take possession of his Earldom until 1336—three years after his father was slain at the Battle of Halidon Hill. In Burk's Peerage this nobleman is described as a man "of great pairts, worth and honour. He joined Robert, the High Steward of Scotland and Governor of the Kingdom, was always steady in his interest, and behaved gallantly on every opportunity against the enemies of his country, and was appointed Justiciar of Scotland benorth the River Fourth."

In 1346, ten years after he succeeded to the Earldom, an unfortunate incident, so far as he was concerned, occurred. King David II. assembled an army at Perth with the view of invading England. Tytler states that the muster was the greatest that had taken place for many years. Troops, he says, were drawn from the Highlands and Islands of Scotland, as well as the Mainland, but, unfortunately, some of the Highland Chiefs brought their petty jealousies with them, which terminated in bloodshed.

The subject of the present notice assassinated Ronald of the Isles along with several of his followers in the Monastery of Elcho, and dreading the Royal vengeance, he led his men back to their home in the Highlands. Ronald, the slain chieftain, it may be explained, was the son of Rory of the Isles, and last male representative of Roderick of Bute—grandson of Somerled of the Isles.

Notwithstanding the desertion of the Earl of Ross with his followers, as well as a number of other Islesmen, the King pressed forward into England, and on the 17th October, 1346, fought the Battle of Durham. The Earl was taken prisoner and sent to the Tower, where he was confined for eleven years.

Nine years later the northern lords had thrown off their allegiance and refused to contribute towards the payment of the King's ransom, which amounted to 100,000 merks—a fabulous sum in those days. Among others who took a leading part in this rebellion was the Earl of Ross and his brother Hugh. No doubt, like so many of the nobility of Scotland, they disapproved of the repeated attempts made on the part of Edward to have Scotland subservient to England, and they took courage from the assistance received from those in power. The Earl, however, had occasion to regret his resolution, and was obliged to find security to keep the peace.

In 1350 the Earl, with the approval of his sister Marjory, Countess of Caithness and Orkney, and upon condition of obtaining the King's concent, appointed his half-brother, Hugh, his heir, On the death of his uncle, Sir John C. Ross, he inherited half of the lands of the Earldom of Buchan.

King David favoured the marriage of the Earl's daughter, Euphemia, with Sir Walter de Leslie, without her father's sanction, and in 1370—probably remembering the Earl's conduct at Elcho—compelled him to resign all his possessions for reinfeftment. His lands were conferred, failing heirs male of his body, upon his daughter Euphemia, and her husband; whom failing, his daughter Janet (who married Sir Alexander Fraser of Cowie) and her heirs.

Upon the death of the Earl of Ross in 1372, the King (David II.) bestowed his daughter Euphemia's hand on Sir Walter Leslie, who became Seventh Earl of Ross. By this union there was a son and daughter—Alexander, who became Earl of Ross, and Margaret, who married Donald, Lord of the Isles.

Euphemia—the Countess of Ross—had led rather a romantic career. There were three main episodes in her life story—(1) Her forced marriage to Sir Walter Leslie;
(2) a similar union with Sir Alexander Stewart, "Wolf of Badenoch," fourth son of Robert II., and (3) her own attempts, after his death, to secure a husband after her own heart.

Her marraige with the "Wolf of Badenoch" was a very unhappy one. His sole object in marrying the Countess was to secure her possessions. In consequence of his unfaithfulness, the Countess had made complaints to the Bishop about his conduct. The Church dignitaries had come to a finding. It proceeds—"We pronounce that Lady Euphemia, Countess of Ross, must be restored to Lord Alexander Senechal, Earl of Buchan and Lord of Ross as her husband and spouse." But, alas for fair promises, Lord Alexander soon relapsed into his old habits, and Countess Euphemia had to seek a separation, and for a time ruled as Countess in her own right.

It was at this period of her life that the third adventure referred to occurred. It appears that she set her eye upon Alexander of Kintail, and that she took the initiative in proposing marriage. The Laird of Kintail, however, refused the proffered offer. Still pressing her suit, she invited him to the Castle of Dingwall, but as he still refused her, she became furious with hate and revenge. Before he realised his position, the Countess had made him prisoner in one of the strong rooms of the Castle of Dingwall.

Kintail's friends in the west, in a roundabout way, became aware of the true state of matters, and the Governor of Ellan-Donan Castle, by the use of strategy, got into communication with his Chief. The Governor was led to understand that nothing could secure the release of the captive but the apprehension of Ross of Balnagown—Ross was a son of a grand-uncle of the Countess. In concern for his master's safety and release, Macaulay the Governor returned without delay to Kintail, and quickly enrolled a goodly number of the Clans Macrae and Mackenzie, and marched eastward, making the fair plains of Easter Ross their objective. The Laird of Balnagown was soon captured, and was brought prisoner along with them. The matter being reported to Lord Lovat, the King's Lieutenant in the North, he lost no time in taking action. He despatched a troop of mounted men from Beaufort, and these were augmented by the Munros of Foulis and others from this locality. The western marauders were overtaken in the valley of the Peffery. Macaulay taking in the situation at a glance, halted, sent Balnagown in charge of a few men westward, and with the remainder waited the oncome of the pursuers. There was a desperate and bloody conflict, made all the more bitter by the presence of so many different clans, who fell upon one another in an indescribable melee. There was great slaughter on both sides. Macaulay, however, had the best of the fight, but Balnagown was released. Young Kintail was set free in exchange for the Governor of Dingwall Castle, sent to Ellandonan by the Countess.

Shortly after this episode the Countess entered the Monastery of Elcho (where her father murdered the eight Islesmen as already referred to). After her death she was buried at Fortrose.

Her eldest son, Alexander, was the Eight Earl of Ross, who married Isabel, eldest daughter of Robert Stewart, Earl of Fife and Duke of Albany, Regent of Scotland, third son of Robert II. The Earl died at Dingwall in 1402, leaving an only child, a daughter called Euphemia, no doubt so named after her grandmother. She illegally resigned the Earldom to her maternal uncle, Sir John Stewart, who therefore styled himself Earl of Buchan and Ross. The rightful heir to the Earldom was Lady Margaret Leslie, sister to the late Earl Alexander, who married Donald, Lord of the Isles. Her husband was not the one to submit to be deprived of the extensive possessions which the Earldom embraced, and his claim being refused he quickly gathered a numerous force, marched through the western mountains, and descended upon Dingwall. He met and defeated Angus Dubh Mackay of Farr and the men of Sutherland, at Dingwall. He afterwards marched through Morayshire and Aberdeenshire, but at Harlaw he was met by the Earl of Mar, an illegitimate son of the "Wolf of Badenoch," at the head of an inferior army in point of numbers, but composed of Lowland gentlemen, who were better armed and better disciplined than were Donald's Highland followers. It was on the 24th July, 1411, the Battle of Harlaw was fought, the result of which was that the Earl was obliged to retire to his Castle at Dingwall, where he shortly afterwards was besiged and forced to yield his pretensions, while, on the other hand, the Earl of Buchan retained the titles and estates of Ross until slain at Vernuil in 1424, when they fell to the Crown.

For some years, James I. retained the Earldom of Ross in his own hands, but in 1427, being minded to put an end to the plottings and troubles that were being set afoot by the Earldom family and their collaterals, the King, at the head of a small force, marched north, and having ordered his Parliament to meet at Inverness, appointed the leading chieftains to meet him there, but specially requesting "his lovit cusins" to appear in his audience chamber in Inverness Castle. The "cusins," Alexander of the Isles and his mother, the Countess of Ross, duly obeyed, but on presenting themselves they were seized and imprisoned. Alexander was soon after liberated, and the first use he made of his liberty was to devastate the Crown lands with a numerous force. He marched on Inverness and burned it, but later, 23rd July, 1429, James defeated him at Lochaber. Being driven from place to place, on 27th August he presented himself before the High Altar at the Chapel of Holyrood, in presence of the King, Queen, and Court, clad only in his under garments, and, giving up his sword, sought for mercy. The King spared his life, but confined him for some months in Tantallon, when his mother and he were released and his lands restored. Alexander died at Dingwall 4th May, 1448. He had married Elizabeth, daughter of Sir Alexander Seton, Lord Gordon and Huntly, and leaving, with other issue, a son John, and two daughters, Margaret and Florence. The eldest daughter married John, Earl of Sutherland, while the second married Lachlan Mackintosh of Mackintosh.

It has been proved beyond doubt that this Earl of Ross had two illegitimate sons, Celestine of Lochalsh, and Hugh, the progenitors of the Macdonalds of Sleat. Indeed they were of age, and married while their brother John, the lawful heir to the Earldom, was still a minor.

John, the last Earl of Ross, had a romantic career, and his line and his reign ended in ignominious eclipse. James II. was actively employed in weakening the power and usurped authority of William, eighth Earl of Douglas. One of this nobleman's most enthusiastic supporters in his rebellious conduct was Livingstone of Callendar. He in turn influenced the young Earl of Ross to join their party, and seized the Royal Castles of Inverness, Urquhart, and Ruthven. An interview between Ross and the new Earl of Douglas, in 1453, resulted in the naval demonstration by the men of the Isles against Ayr. This expedition was under the command of his kinsman, Donald Balloch of the Isles. Owing, however, to the able measures of defence adopted by the King, the enterprise met with little success.

The Earl of Douglas returned to England after the failure of this expedition, and the Earl of Ross, finding himself alone in rebellion, became alarmed for the consequences, and by a submissive message entreated the forgiveness of the King, offering as far as it was still left to him to repair the wrongs he had inflicted. James at first refused to listen to the application, but, after a time, consented to extend to the humble chief a period of probation, within which, if he should evince the reality of his repentance by some noble exploit, he was to be absolved from all the consequences of his rebellion and reinstated in the Royal favour.

The Earl of Ross was, in 1457, one of the Wardens of the Marches, an office of great trust and importance, but obviously intended to weaken his influence in the Highlands and Isles, by forcing him frequently to reside at a distance from the seat of power, and, as he was one of the nobles who guaranteed a truce with England, it would seem that he had lost no time in effecting a reconciliation with the King.

Previous to the seige of Roxburgh, at which James II. was killed, the Earl of Ross joined the Royal Army with a body of three thousand of his vassals. In order to prove his fidelity and loyalty he offered, in case of invasion of England, to precede the rest of the army, while in the enemy's country, by a thousand paces distance, so as to receive the first shock of the English. Ross was well received and ordered to remain near the King's person, but as there was at this time no invasion of England, the courage and devotion of himself and his troops were not put to the test.

In 1462 the Earl made an Independent treaty with Edward IV., the English King, along with the Earl of Douglas, whereby they became his vassals. Edward was in return to assist them to conquer Scotland, which was then to be partitioned between the Earls and Donald Balloch. The Earl of Ross was not slow to carry this resolution into effect. He sent his bastard son, Angus,

and his half-brother, Celestine, to conquer Inverness and Moray, which commission they carried into effect.
How this extraordinary rebellion was suppressed is uncertain. It is known that the Earl of Ross was summoned before Parliament to answer to a charge of treason, and that on his failing to appear his Earldom was forfeited to the Crown for ever. He was then partially restored, with remainder to his illegitimate sons, being made a Lord of Parliament under the style of John de Isla, Lord of the Isles.

The Lord of the Isles, having lost the Earldom estates, was still pursued by evil fortune, for he was deprived of his estates by his lawless son, Angus, and on account of the turbulent proceedings then going on in the Highlands, he was once again summoned before the King and charged with treason. That was in April, 1478. He, however, soon satisfied the Government of his innocence and at the same time procured the pardon of his son. While at Inverness, however, doing battle against the Mackenzies, Angus was assassinated by an Irish harper, so that by his death the lineage of John, the last Lord of the Isles, was wiped out.

On the death of his heir, the aged Lord of the Isles once again resumed possession of his estates, from which for some time he had been excluded by the unnatural violence of his son Angus. The right of heir to the Lordship was now held by his nephew, Alexander of Lochalsh, son of his brother Celestine, and eventually the "Lord of the Isles,. . . . allied on equal terms with England's pride," died in the Abbey of Paisley in 1498, having retired from the tumult and excitement of the times in which he lived, and at his own request, was buried in the tomb of his Royal ancestor, King Robert II.

After the death of John, the last Earl of Ross, a Dukedom of Ross was created by James III. in favour of his son James, who resigned the estates from which he derived his title in 1503, and, some years later, Alexander, the posthumous son of James IV., was created Earl of Ross.

In 1503 Donald Dubh, natural son of Angus, above referred to, set up claims to the latter dignity, but was taken prisoner. After forty years' confinement he escaped, and in 1544 rose once more in rebellion, assumed the titles of Ross and the Isles, and entered into a treaty with Edward, but died at Drogheda the following year.

Between 1503 and 1544 several futile attempts were made to recover the Lordship of Ross, and the Bishop of Caithness, as Chamberlain of Ross, had to hold the Castles of Dingwall and Redcastle against the men of the Isles and others who had pretensions to the Castle and the Earldom lands.

The line of Lochalsh terminated with two daughters, one of whom, Margaret, married Alexander of Glengarry, while the second became the wife of Dingwall of Kildun. As a consequence of this failure of male descendents of Celestine, Donald Gorm, the representative of the kindred illegitimate house of Sleat, appeared as the next claimant for the Earldom. In 1562, Donald followed Mary, Queen of Scots, everywhere, begging that he might have the Earldom conferred upon him. He was, however, disappointed, and, according to the usual custom, flew to the English and entered into a treaty with them, which, however, came to nought.

The Earldom was revived in 1565, when, on the 25th of May, Henry Stewart (Lord Darnley) was created Earl of Ross, and on the 22nd July of the same year the Banns of Marriage were proclaimed between "Harie, Earl of Ross," and Queen Mary. It will thus be seen that the unfortunate Darnley was the last to enjoy the Earldom.

AEneas Macdonell of Glengarry became a claimant for the dignity—the grounds of his pretensions being that his great-great-grandfather had married the granddaughter of the illegitimate Celestine of Lochalsh. Glengarry was ready to go anywhere and do anything for Charles I., provided he was made Earl of Ross. On the 30th of July, 1646, he wrote to King Charles from Castle Leod, professing loyalty and obedience, "being only desyrus that your Majesty may kno of a particulare faithful servand to receive and act your commands." At the Restoration, on account of his services, he was created Lord Macdonell and Aros by King Charles II., who, it seems by certain documents, had granted several warrants creating him Earl of Ross, but these did not take effect.

There was another, and last, claimant to the Earldom— Lord Ross of Hawkhead, who is referred to hereafter among the Rosses of Balnagown. Obviously he had no connection with the Earldom, and a rather scathing dismissal of his pretensions is contained in a Letter written by Lord Tarbat of the period, in which he goes in to say that, while Lord Ross had no direct connection with the Earls—"no more relation to them, directly or indirectly, than the miller of Carstares has to the Prince of Parma"—"there are very considerable families have parts of this Earldom of Ross. . . . such are the Earls of Seaforth, and several other considerable heritors. . . . the Earl of Cromartie, Rosehaugh, Scatwell, Gairloch, Coul, Redcastle, Culcoy, Fowles, Culrain, Kilravock, Cadboll, Fairburn, Tulloch, Macleod of Lewis, Macdonald of Mackenzie of Suddie, many of which does not think my Lord Ross fit to be their superior." Nothing came of the Hawkhead claim.

PERSONAL ARMS OF THE
HEAD OF THE HOUSE OF ROSS OF BALNAGOWN

Rosses of Balnagown

The Rosses of Balnagown were for centuries the oldest branch of the line. Fraser-Mackintosh in "Antiquarian Notes" points out that in 1338 "John Ross of Balnagown" is witness to a deed granted by one of the Lords of the Isles, and signed at Kessack. In later years various settlements were proposed for establishing the succession to the broad lands of Balnagown, which, by a document registered at Fortrose in 1688, consisted of forty-eight properties.

In Gordon's "History of the Earldom of Sutherland," the following reference, already quoted, is made to the origin of the Balnagown family of Rosses:—"From the second son of the Earl of Ross the lands of Balnagown are descended, and had by inheritance the lands of Rarichies and Colluigh (Cullise) where you may observe that the laird of Balnagown his sirname should not be Ross, seeing there never was any Earl of Ross of that name, but the Earls of Ross were first of the sirname Builion, then they were Leslies, and last of all that Earldom fell by inheritance to the Lords of the Isles, who resigned the same into King James III. his lands, the year of God 1477. So I do think that the lairds of Balnagown, perceiving the Earls of Ross decayed, and that Earldom fallen into the Lords of the Isles' hands, they called themselves Rosses, thereby to testify their descent from the Earls of Ross. Besides all the Rosses in that Provence are into this day called in (Gaelic) language Clan andris, which race, by their own tradition, is sprung from another stock."

I., Hugh Ross of Rarichies became first of Balnagown. He obtained these and other lands by a grant from his brother. He was the third son of Hugh, Earl of Ross, being the eldest son of the Earl's second marriage with Margaret Graham, daughter of Sir David Graham of Old Montrose. He was married to Margaret Baclay and had issue—(1) William, (2) Jean, who married Robert Munroe, eighth Baron of Foulis.

II., William, as a matter of course, succeeded his father in the lands and became second laird of Balnagown. He married Christina, daughter of Lord Livingstone. In

Reid's "Earls of Ross," this lady is credited with having built the Kirk of Alness, or, according to another account, the Bridge of Alness. They were succeeded by their son, III., Walter, third of Balnagown. Besides the lands of Balnagown, he was granted the lands of Cullisse, in the parish of Nigg, by Alexander Leslie, Earl of Ross. He married Catherine, daughter of Paul Mactyre, the freebooter. This Paul is represented to be the grandson of a Norwegian invader of Royal rank, who made his name a terror, as Rob Roy in his day in the Southern Highlands. In the Chronicles of the Earls of Ross he is described as "a very takand man, which means taking away by force men's goods, and cattle and lands, so that he made himself owner of a large part of Sutherland and the parish of Kincardine in the County of Ross."

In Taylor's "History of Tain" it is stated that "this 'gentleman' became so powerful that the family of Balnagown appear to have been fain to give him a daughter of their house in marriage, and along with her a legal grant of the lands of Kincardine, which he had already seized." We cannot find confirmation of this in the records. On the contrary, it appears that the laird of Balnagown of that day, as mentioned above, married Paul's daughter, and as a dowry he gave her the lands of Strathcarron, Strathoykell, and Westray. They left issue, a son,

IV., Hugh, fourth of Balnagown, who is, on the authority of the Chronicles of the Earls of Ross, credited with having married a daughter of the Earl of Sutherland, by his wife, Helen Sinclair, daughter of the Earl of Orkney, but there is no confirmation of this union to be found in the pedigrees of the House of Sutherland. They had issue—(1) John, who became fifth of Balnagown; (2) William of Little Allan, who became first of Shandwick; (3) Thomas, who became Sub-Dean of Ross and Rector of the Collegiate Church of Tain:

V., John, fifth of Balnagown, was married to Christina, a daughter of Torquil Macleod of the Lewis. They had issue—(1) Alexander, who became sixth of Balnagown: (2) Donald, who became first of Priesthill and Dean of Caithness, and three other sons.

VI., Alexander, sixth of Balnagown, married Dorothy, daughter of Alexander Sutherland of Duffus. Gordon, in his "Earldom of Sutherland," describes a bloody encounter which took place between John, Earl of Sutherland, and this Alexander, at Alt Charrais. He gives the date of this battle as the 11th of July, 1487, while the Callendar of Fearn gives it as June, 1486.

The occasion of the battle, it would appear, was revenge. One Alexander Mackay, the son of Neil Gald, or Neil Wasse-Mackay, had been previously slain at Tarbat. A son of the slain man begged the Earl of Sutherland for assistance so that he might be revenged for his father's death. The Earl yielded, and sent his uncle, Robert Sutherland, with a company of chosen men to assist Mackay. Strathoykell was invaded with fire and sword, and there was "burnt, spoiled, and wasted many lands appertaining to the Rosses. The laird of Balnagown hearing of this invasion, gathered all the forces of the Provence of Ross, and met Robert Sutherland and John Mackay at a place called Alt Charrais. The fight continued for a long space, with incredible obstinacy: the doubt of the victory being no less great than was the desire. Much blood was shed. In the end, the inhabitants of Ross, being unable to endure the enemy's forces, were disbanded and put to flight. Alexander Ross, laird of Balnagown, was there slain, with seventeen other landed gentlemen of the Provence of Ross, besides a great number of common soldiers."

The Kalendar of Fearn furnishes the names of some of these, viz,;— Alexander Ross of Balnagown, William Ross, Alexander Tarrell, Angus Macculloch of Tarrell, William Ross, John Wasse (Vass), John Mitchell, Thomas Wause Vass, Hutchion Vause (Vass).

Alexander left issue—(1) David, who became seventh of Balnagown, and (2) Isobell, who married, as his first wife, George Munroe, tenth of Foulis.

VII., David, on the death of his father, became seventh laird of Balnagown. He was twice married (1) to Helen Keith, daughter of the Duke of Albany. For some reason unknown, this laird was made a Knight, probably through the patronage of his second wife. By his first wife he had a family— (1) Walter, who became eighth of Balnagown; (2) William, who became first of Invercharron; (3) Hugh, who became first of Tolly and Achnacloich; (4) Angus, who married the daughter of

William Macculloch of Plaids.

VIII., Walter, eighth of Balnagown, according to the Kalendar of Fearn, was slain at Tain in 1528. He was married to Marion, daughter of Sir John James Grant of Grant, and had issue—(1) Alexander; (2) Katherine, who married John Denoon of Cadboll, one of the magistrates of Tain; (3) Janet, who married the fifth Lord Lovat.

The family of Denune (Denoon) is of great antiquity in Scotland. It is an Argyleshire name, and can be traced back to the time of Alexander III. The first of the name to settle in Easter Ross was Donald, who was an Abbot of the Abbey of Fearn, and acquired considerable wealth. The lands of Cadboll, which at one time were Abbey lands, passed into his hands. He was succeeded in this property by Andrew Denoon, his nephew, second laird of Cadboll of that name. That was in the year 1534. Contemporary with this Andrew lived Sir David Denoon, who possessed considerable property in the parish of Tain, viz., the Barony of Pitogarty, Pitnellies, Balnacouth. Andrew of Cadboll died in the reign of Queen Mary, leaving a son, John, who became third of Cadboll. It was to the latter that Katherine, referred to above, was married. The marriage deed is dated 12th April, 1556.

It is of interest to state that, although the lands of Cadboll have changed hands several times during the past three centuries, there are quite a number of families who bear the surname (Denoon) living in the north of Scotland, but more particularly in Easter Ross, who, no doubt, are descendants of this ancient family. In the Fendum, near Tain, on the very spot where Sir Andrew Denoon owned lands, are several families of the same name who have lived there from time immemorial, so that the presumption is that they are the descendants of the Baronet of that name who flourished there centuries ago.

IX., Alexander, ninth of Balnagown, was married (1) to Janet, daughter of John, third Earl of Caithness, and (2) to Catherine, daughter of Kenneth Mackenzie of Kintail. By his first wife he had issue—(1) Robert; (2) Hector; (3) George, who became tenth of Balnagown; (4) Catherine; (5) Agnes, who married Duncan Campbell of Boath; (6) Christian, who married Kenneth Mackenzie, third of Dochmaluack. By the second wife he had issue—(1)

Nicholas, who became first laird of Pitcalnie; (2) Malcolm, who died without issue.

Alexander was confined in the Castle of Tantallon for his avowed opposition to the reigning monarch, James VI., but was afterwards set at liberty. He died at Ardmore in 1592, and was buried with his kith and kin at Fearn. His eldest daughter, Katherine, had rather an unenviable career, the particulars of which are set forth in Chambers' Domestic Annals of Scotland (volume I., page 203), and, although the digression is lengthy, it will throw a flood of light upon the belief in superstition and witchcraft entertained in those days. Says Chambers:—

"Her husband and his eldest son were dead when, sometime after, she and Hector, then representative of the family, were tried separately for sundry offences. Hector being, strange to say, the private pursuer against his stepmother, although he had immediately after to take his own place at the bar as a criminal. The dittay against the lady set forth a series of attempts at serious crime, partly procured by natural means and partly by superstitious practices. It appears that she desired to put her eldest stepson out of the way, not, as might have been supposed, to favour the sucession of her own offspring, but that her brother, George Ross of Balnagown, might be free to marry Robert Munro's wife; to which end she also took steps for the removal of the wife of George Ross. It appears that she was not only prompted to but assisted in her attempts by George himself, although no judicial notice was taken of his criminality. Catherine Ross, described as a daughter of Sir David Ross of Balnagown, was also concerned.

"Having formed her design sometime in the year 1576, Lady Foulis opened negotiations with various wretched persons in her neighbourhood who practiced witchcraft, and first with one named William MacGillivray, whom she feed with a present of linen cloth, and afterwards with sums of money. One Angus Roy, a notorious witch (wizard), was sent by her to secure the services of a particularly potent sorceress, named Marion McKean McAllister, or more commonly Lasky Loncart, who was brought to Foulis and lodged with Christina Ross Malcolmson, that she might assist with her diabolic arts. Christina, too, was sent to Dingwall to bring John McNillan, who appears to have been a wizard of note. Another named Thomas McKean McAllan McEndrick was taken into Counsel, besides whom there were a few subordinate instruments. Some of the horrible crew being assembled at Canorth, images of the young laird of Foulis, and the young Lady Balnagown were formed of butter, set upon, and shot at by Lasky Loncart with an elf arrow—that is one of those flint arrowheads which are occasionally found, and believed by the ignorant to be Fairy weapons, while in reality they are relics of our savage ancestors. The shot was repeated eight times, but without hitting the images, so this was regarded as a failure.

"On another day images of clay were set up and shot at twelve times yet equally without effect. Linen cloth had been provided, wherewith to have swathed the images in the event of their being hit, after which they would have been interred under the bridge-end of the tank of Foulis. The subject of all these proceedings was, of course, to produce the destruction of the persons represented by the images. This plan being ineffectual, Lady Foulis and her brother are described as soon after holding a meeting in a kiln at Drimuin to arrange about further procedure. The result was a resolution to try the more direct means of poison with both the obnoxious persons. A stoup of poisoned ale was prepared and set aside, but was nearly all lost by a leak in the vessel. Lady Foulis then procured from Lasky Loncart a pipkin of ranker poison, which she sent to young Munroe by her nurse on purpose to have destroyed him. It fell by the way and broke, when the nurse tasting the liquor was immediately killed by it. It was said that the place where the pig (pipkin) broke the gerse that grew upon the same was so heich lye (beyond) the nature of other gerse, that neither cow nor sheep ever previt (tasted) thereof yet, whilk is manifest and nortorious to the haill Country of Ross."

Lady Foulis was accused of afterwards making renewed attempts, not merely to poison young Munroe, but many of his relations, particularly those who stood in the way of her own son's succession. There seems, however, to have been no success in this quarter.

Matters turned out better with the innocent young Lady Balnagown. Regarding her, Lady Foulis is represented as thus expressing herself, that "she would do by all kind of means, wherever it might be had, of God in heaven, or the devil in hell, for the destruction and down putting of Marjory Campbell." By corrupting a cook, Lady Foulis contrived that some rat poison should be administered to her victim in a dish of kids' kidneys. Catherine Niven, who had brought the poison "scunnerit (revolted) with it sae meikle, that she said it was the sairest and maist cruel sight that ever she saw, seeing the vomit and vexation that was on the young Lady Balnagown and her company." By vomiting, death seems to have been evaded, but the lady contracted, in consequence, what is described at the trial as an incurable illness.

Not long after these events, they became the subject of Judicial investigation, and Christina Ross and Thomas McKean were apprehended, brought to trial, convicted, and burnt, November 1577.

It is alleged that a few days before they suffered, Lady Foulis came into their presence and, referring to the common reports against her, accusing her of sorcery and poisoning, declared herself ready to abide a trial, when, there being no one present to accuse her, she asked instruments to that effect, after which, mounting a horse which had been kept ready, she rode away to Caithness, and remained there three-quarters of a year. By the intercession of the Earl of Caithness, she was then taken back by her husband, and there seems to have been no further notice of her case for several years.

At length, in 1589, her husband being dead, his successor, Robert Munroe, purchased a commission for the trial of certain witches and sorcerers, aiming evidently at retribution upon his wicked stepmother. According to the dittay: "Before any publication thereof, and ere he might have convenient time to put the same in execution, in respects of the troubles that occured in the North, thou, knowing thyself guilty, and fearing to bide the trial of ane assize fand the moyen (found the means) to purchase ane suspension of the said Commission, and caused insert in the said suspension, not only thine ane name and sic others as was specified in the said Commission, but also certain others who were not spoken of . . . . whilk, gif thou had been ane honest woman, and willing to abide trial, thou wald never have causit suspension of any sic Commission, but wald rather have furtherit the same." In the same year Robert Munro died, under what circumstances does not appear, leaving the succession to his brother Hector, who now appeared as nominal prosecutor of his stepmother.

In the circumstances under which the trial took place, the jury being a packed one of humble dependants of the Foulis family, a conviction was not to be expected, Lady Foulis was "pronounced to be innocent and quit of the haill points of the dittay, whereupon she asked instruments."

The dittay against Hector Munroe of Foulis sets forth sundry affairs of necromancy, in which he was alleged to have been concerned along with reputed sorcerers. He had in August, 1588, communed with three notorious witches for the recovery of his elder brother, the then young laird. For this purpose they "pullit the hair of Robert Munroe, and plet the nails of the fingers and taes," seeking by these devilish means to have cured him of his "sickness." Meeting with no success, they told him he had been too late in sending for them. He, for fear of his father, conveyed them away under silence of night. Having himself taken sickness in the ensuing January, while lying at a house in Alness, he had Marion McIngarroch, a notorious witch, brought to him for the purpose of obtaining the benefit of her skill. "She, after her coming to you," says the dittay, "gave you three drinks of water forth of three stanes, which she had: and, after long consultation had with her, she disbarit that there was nae remedy for you to recover your health, without the principal man of your blude should suffer death for you." Having pitched upon his half-brother George, he sent for him from the hunting, and, "as a means of working his destruction, gave his left hand into George's right hand, taking care at the same time not to be the first to speak, That night, at one o'clock after midnight, the said witch, with certain of her complices, passed forth of the house where he lay, and took with them spades, and passed to ane piece of earth, lying betwixt twa sundry superior's lands. . . . . and made ane grave of your length, and took up the ower (upper) part thereof, and laid it aside: the said earth being near the sea-flood. And, this being done, she came hame and convenit certain of your familiars, that knew their part, in taking of you forth to be beardit in the foresaid grave, for your relief, and to the death of your brother George. . . . Whaes (that is the accused) answer was, that giff George should depart suddenly, the bruit (report) wald rise, and all their lives would be in danger: and therefore willet her to delay the said George's death ane space: and she took in hand to warrent him into the 17th day of April next thereafter. And after their plats laid by the said witch, she and certain of your servants. . . . put you in ane pair blankets, and carried you forth to the said grave. And they were all commanded to be dumb and never to speak ane word, into the time that she and your foster-mother should first speak with her master the devil. And being brought forth (you) was laid in the same grave: and the green earth which was cutit, was laid aboon, and halden down with stanes, the said witch being beside you. . . . Christian Neill, your foster-mother, was commanded to run the bredth of nine rigs, and in her hand, younger Hector Leith's son. And how soon Christian had run the bredth of the nine rigs, she came again to the grave, an enquired at the said witch, 'Whilk was her choice?' Wha answered and said, that Mr Hector was her choice to live, and your brother George was to die for you.

And this form was used thrice that night: and therefore ye was carried hame, all the company being dumb, and was put in your bed."

Contrary to what one would expect of an invalid exposed in this manner on a January night, Hector Munro recovered. His brother George took ill in April, 1590, and lingered to the beginning of July, when he died. No doubt being entertained that his mortal illness was caused by witchcraft, his mother, the subject of the previous trial, appears to have immediately summoned a prosecution against Hector, now laird; and the result was a trial following immediately that in which he had appeared as prosecutor against her. This trial had the same issue as the other, the jury being composed in a similar manner.

This Catherine was the mother of a numerous family, which included (1) George, who became first laird of Obesdale (Obsdale) of the name of Munro; (2) John of Meikle Davanch.

X., George, tenth of Balnagown, succeeded to the property in May, 1560. Later he got the lands of Easter Fearn and Mulderg. He was educated at St. Andrews, but nothing eventful occured in his life save, perhaps, having assisted the Mackenzies in their contention with the Macdonalds of Glengarry.

George was twice married, first to Marion, daughter of Sir John Campbell of Calder (Cawdor). In the "Thanes of Cawdor" there is recorded a contract dated 30th August, 1572, which bears "that the Lady Murial's grandson, John Campbell, apparent heir of Cawdor, and her sons, Donald of Ichterachyn, and Duncan of Boyth, bound themselves for the part remaining unpaid of the tocher of

300 merks, covenanted to be paid by Dame Muriel with her daughter Margory, the spouse of George Ross of Balnagown."

By this marriage he had issue—(1) David, who became eleventh of Balnagown, and four daughters. The eldest, Jean, married Kenneth, first Lord of Kintail. In Mackenzie's History of the Mackenzies this lady is called Ann. There was born of this marriage (1) Colin, who afterwards became first Earl of Seaforth; (2) John of Lochslin; (3) Kenneth, who died unmarried.

The second daughter, Catherine, was married to Sir William Sinclair of Mey. The third, Mariella, married Duncan Grant, son of Patrick Grant of Rothiemurchus; while the fourth daughter, Isabell, married John Munro, first of Fearn.

George married, secondly, Isobell, second daughter of Angus Mackintosh of Mackintosh. He had also a natural son, Alexander. He was succeeded by his eldest son,

XI., David, eleventh of Balnagown. He was married to Lady Mary Gordon, second daughter of Alexander, Earl of Sutherland, who is described in Gordon's Earldom of Sutherland as a "virtuous and comely woman, lady of ane excellent and quick wit." She died without issue at Overskibo, and was buried at Dornoch.

By David's marriage contract with his wife it was arranged that, should there be a failure of an heir male to Balnagown, then John, Master of Sutherland, should marry Jean, eldest daughter of George.

David married, secondly, Lady Annabella Murray, daughter of John, Earl of Tullibardine, and had issue an only son, who succeeded his father as twelfth laird of Balnagown.

David died on the 20th November 1632, and was buried in the family vault in the Abbey of Fearn.

XII., David, twelfth of Balnagown, succeeded to the ancestral estates of his father while yet a young man. At his own expense he raised a regiment of his clan and proceeded to the fatal battle of Worcester, which was fought in 1651. On that occasion, it will be recalled, the Scots army went to England in order, if possible, to reinstate Charles II., but they were defeated by Cromwell, who called the battle his "crowning mercy." Charles with difficulty escaped to France. More than 2000 of the

Royalists were slain, and of 8000 prisoners, the greater part were sold as slaves to the American colonists.

The laird of Balnagown was taken, and committed to the Tower, and after being imprisoned there for some years died, and was buried at Westminster on the 29th December, 1653.

This sacrifice on the part of Balnagown was not forgotten by Charles II. when his opportunity came, for it is recorded that he settled a pension on his son.

He was married to Marie, eldest daughter of Hugh, Lord Fraser of Lovat. She died at Ardmore 22nd December, 1646, leaving issue—(1) David, who became thirteenth and last laird of Balnagown of the old family; (2) Alexander, who died at the age of twenty; (3) Isobell, who was married to James Innes of Lightness, brother to Sir Robert Innes of that ilk; (4) Catherine, who married John Mackenzie, fourth of Inverlaul.

XIII., David, thirteenth of Balnagown, succeeded to the estate after his father's death, and during the lifetime of the latter laird one of the most eventful chapters in connection with property-seizing of which there is any record in the annals of Highland history was perpetrated.

This David was a weak man, and was entirely under the control of a strong-minded wife. To aggravate matters, not only in the time of the laird of the time, but also that of his father, the lands of Balnagown became very much encumbered, which state of affairs gave much anxiety to friends of the family. This is illustrated by a quaint letter of the Earl of Mar's which is preserved in the "Kilravock Papers." While that was so, it afforded an excellent opportunity to covetous parties to resort to questionable means to get possession of the property.

Shaw, the historian of the Province of Moray, furnishes some details as to the state of matters which existed on the Balnagown property at the time referred to. From pages 310-311 of this interesting work the following passage is reproduced:—

In the year 1683, William Lord Ross stood infeft in the lands and estate of Balnagown, upon a Charter under the Great Seal to him and his heirs male. And in 1647, Robert Lord Ross, as heir to his brother was infeft therein: and in 1648, Lord Robert resigned in favour of David of Balnagown, and the heirs male of his body, which failing to revert to Lord Robert, and thereon David was infeft. This David upon his own charges, brought a battalion of his name to the fatal battle of Worcester anno 1651, was himself made prisoner, and died at Windsor about the year 1667, which swelled the debts of the family so much, that though his son David served heir to him in 1658, and married Ann Stuart, sister to Alexander Earl of Murray, yet he was scon obliged to wadset lands to the value of £5000 sterling. And in 1680 Ross of Morangie apprised the whole estate for debt and his assigney Roderick Dingwall, was in 1685 infeft upon a charter under the Great Seal passed upon this apprising. And there were other apprisings besides this.

To prevent the effects of these apprisings, and there being no hopes of Balnagown's having issue, a transcation was made, of date 22nd May, 1685, betwixt Balnagown and Alexander, Earl of Murray, for conveying the estate to Francis Stuart, son of the said Earl, by which the Earl advanced £ 10,000 Scots to David, and David resigned the estate to himself in lifetime, and to the said Mr Francis in fee, and to other heirs therein named.

The procuratory of resignation contained a redemption in favour of David and heirs of his body on payment of the £10,000 Scots and interest, and what other sum may be advanced to David and his creditors: and Mr Francis should assume the sirname and arms of the family after David's demise.

In consequence of this transaction, Mr Francis, before the year 1706, was creditor to Balnagown in 63,000 merks, and bound with him in 8000 Scots to Roderick Dingwall,£ 8000 merks to Inverchaslie (Invercasley) and 1400 to Suttie, which exeeded the value of the lands not wadsetted, of liferented by the Lady: and so Mr Francis was loser, and ready to repudiate and reduce a deed done for him when he was a child.

Upon this, Mr Francis, in the year 1706, with Balnagown's consent, conveyed the estate to Lord Ross, and the heirs male of his body (reserving still the liferent),which failing, to such as Balnagown would appoint.

And Lord Ross advanced to Mr Francis 63,000 merks, and an obligation to relieve him of all debts for which he stood bound on that estate, and Lord Ross was infefted in 1707.

Thereafter, in 1771, Lord Ross, and his son George, with consent of Balnagown conveyed the estate to Lieut.-General Charles Ross, his heirs and assigns reserving the lifetime: for which he paid to Lord Ross £ 3500 stg., and was infeft by a charter under the Great Seal in 1713. He redeemed the wadsets: and David of Balnagown dieing in 1716, and his lady in 1719, the General got full possession, and in 1727 settled the estate on his grand-nephew, Captain Charles Ross, who, upon the General's death in 1732, was infeft anno 1734. Thus was the estate of Balnagown conveyed to another family.

David died on the 17th April, 1711, and his property passed, as may be seen from the foregoing extract, to another family of Rosses, but in no way connected with the Balnagown line.

It was only natural that the next heirs of the blood should endeavour to recapture the estate from the possession of strangers. The nearest heir male was Mr Ross of Pitcalnie. He rested his claim on two grounds—first, that David Ross, the last of the old Balnagown family, possessed under letters of entail; and, secondly, that he was so weak minded as to have been susceptible of undue influence. Fraser-Mackintosh in his "Letters of Two Centuries" states that "in the annals of Scotland there is, perhaps, no greater case of fraud and wrong than the unscrupulous, but ultimately successful attempts of Lord Ross, and General Charles Ross, strangers to the family, to possess themselves of the estate of Balnagown."

In the course of that memorable trial it came out that the late laird was not only weak minded, under the influence of his wife, but also under the influence of his brother-in-law, the Earl of Moray, his wife's brother.

Lady Ross, on the contrary, is handed down to posterity by a contributor in the "New Statistical Account" as a person "endowed no less with the gifts of nature than with those of grace. . . . She bequeathed the sum of 3000 merks Scots for behoof of some indigent persons fearing the Lord in the County of Ross." But her conduct in endeavouring to influence her husband to make the estate over to her brother will scarcely bear out this fulsome eulogy. One of her chief advisers was the Rev. William Stewart, Presbyterian minister of Kiltearn. A very different man, as Mr Fraser-Mackintosh points out, to his predecessor, "Godly Mr Hogg."

It appears that this eccentric laird of Balnagown was appointed Governor of the town of Inverness, in the latter part of the seventeenth century, and consequently had to live for periods in that town. At the trial referred to, quite a number of Inverness personages, who knew the laird, were called as witnesses, and their deposition is preserved in "Antiquarian Notes."

Among a series of complaints, writes Mr Fraser-Mackintosh there, against Balnagown in the year 1694, on the part of some of his clan, the following is somewhat singular, viz.:—"That Balnagown never keeps burials or public meetings in the shire, and it is generally said and reported that it is for fear of the Master of Tarbat that he withdraws from both."

As will be inferred from the passage already quoted from Shaw, the relatives of Lady Ross figured conspicuously in their efforts to secure possession of Balnagown. On the 20th of July, 1688, the laird of Balnagown obtained a charter to himself and Francis Stuart of the lands and Barony of Balnagown. The heir to the Earldom of Moray having died, Francis became heir-apparent to the Earldom, and among the country people strong dissatisfaction began to be felt at the idea of the lands becoming an appendage of the Earldom, and Francis Stuart, it would appear, did not overpress his claim. It was alleged that the Earl of Moray, in respect of his son's ultimate succession, advanced money to Balnagown to assist him to pay his debts, but this Pitcalnie denied.

In the year 1694 a new claimant appears on the scene in the person of William Lord Ross. He relied on the fact, according to Shaw, "that in the year 1688 he stood infeft in the lands and estates of Balnagown upon a Charter under the Great Seal to him and his heirs male. In 1647, Robert Lord Ross, as heir to his brother, was infeft therein; and in 1648, Lord Robert resigned in favour of David of Balnagown (the father of the thirteenth laird) and the heirs male of his body, which failing, to revert to Lord Robert," but this lacks confirmation.

The accounts of Lady Ross's endeavours to secure Balnagown are highly interesting. It seems that Lady Ross was displeased with the people for being prejudiced against her brother, which made Lord Ross more determined than ever to accomplish his object. In a letter to Hugh Rose of Kilravock (who was on friendly terms with the Balnagown family), Lady Ann was promised a Countess's Coronet if she would only assist him to accomplish his object. It was already pointed out that Lady Ann was much under the influence of a certain clergyman named Stewart. In a letter from Lord Ross to

George Ross of Morangie, dated January 1700, he says, still quoting from "Antiquarian Notes":—"Receive also enclosed a letter to Kilravock, another to Mr Stewart, which you may read, seal, and deliver, and take all the effectual methods you can by Mr Stewart to get it effectual with the lady, and acquaint me sometimes what success ye expect, and, I do assure you, I will gratify you on the success handsomely." And again—"But pray desire Mr Stewart to be earnest to put this affair to an end. I wish it may be to satisfaction. Impress upon Mr Stewart how great advantage it were to the Presbyterian interest there that I had an interest in Balnagown, since I had been so forward to that interest. Whereas if a Popish family came in, it may ruin that interest there. Kilravock and ye on the place can use many more arguments than I know, particularly that if Balnagown were dead, the name will never submit to a Stuart."

To Mr Stewart himself Lord Ross writes the same day:—"I am informed ye have a considerable interest with Lady Balnagown. If you will be so kind as to use your interest with the lady to get my affair succeed, I do assure you, I will never fail in my occasion wherein I can serve you, and if thereby you bring me to an interest in that country, ye will thereby put me in a condition to serve you more effectually."

This is pretty plain, and it would appear to have been at once successful, though one of two who first saw it considered it rather "distinct," and that the minister would need a little preliminary "dealing."

In Mr Stewart's answer, dated Kiltearn, 6th February, 1700, he says, after acknowledging receipt:—"After mature thoughts thereanent, I am fully persuaded and inclined to judge it my duty to obtemper your lordship's desire." And again—"It is true I see some difficulties in the undertaking, not with respect to duty but success, which your lordship may easily conjecture, but on the grounds above mentioned, and because success and events belong to the Lord, I shall use such means, leaving it to the Lord— whose sovereign providence has the determining hand in all the actions and transactions here below— to dispose of the event."

The estates of Balnagown accordingly descended to the said Lord Ross, but, for some unexplainable reason, he infefted his brother, General Charles Ross, into the property. The latter having no family of his own, entailed his properties upon the children of his sister, the Hon. Grizel Ross, wife of Sir James Lockhart of Carstairs, whose second son, Colonel Sir James Ross, accordingly succeeded.

By the provisions of his uncle's will, Captain John Lockhart, his younger brother, obtained the property, and took the name of Ross in addition to his own.

THE LOCHART-ROSSES OF BALNAGOWN

The first of the lineage was William, second son of Sir James Lockhart of Lee, who received his Knighthood from James VI. He was succeeded by his grandson,

I., William Lockhart of Lockhart Hall, in the County of Lanark, who was created a Baronet of Nova Scotia on the 26th February, 1672. The Baronet died in 1710, and was succeeded by his son,

II., Sir James Lockhart, who was married to Grizel, third daughter of William, 12th Lord Ross, and had a family of six sons. The property descended to the eldest son, William.

III., Sir William Lockhart succeeded his father on the 31st July, 1755. He was twice married—first to Miss Agnew, and secondly to Catherine, daughter of John Porterfield of Fullwood, by whom he had two daughters. Sir William died in June 1758, when the title devolved upon his brother,

IV., Sir James Lockhart of Lanark. Sir James married a daughter of Major John Croslie, but dying in September 1760, without issue, was succeeded by his brother George.

V., Sir George Lockhart was unmarried, and after possessing the estate for eighteen years died, and was succeeded by his younger brother, John.

VI., Sir John Lockhart-Ross was the fifth son of Sir James Lockhart, and was born at Lockhart Hall, Lanarkshire, on the 11th November, 1721. At an early age he manifested an inclination for the sea, and accordingly he was allowed to join the Navy service in his fourteenth year. He became a distinguished Naval officer, and in 1756 was placed in command of the "Tartar," a frigate of 24 guns, in which he rendered gallant service for his Sovereign and his country during those memorable times. In the course of fifteen months, he captured in the British Channel nine of the enemy's ships of war, several of them, it is recorded, being of superior force. He was promoted to the rank of Vice-Admiral of the Blue. By the death of his brother, Sir George, which took place in July 1778, the Baronetcy of the family descended to him, as well as the estate of his maternal uncle, General Ross. He also <u>assumed</u> the additional <u>name of Ross</u>, and the estate of Lochart being sold in 1762, he adopted the designation "of Balnagown."

Sir John Lockhart-Ross was married to Elizabeth, only daughter of Robert Dundas of Arniston, Lord-President of the Court of Session from 1760 to 1788. After the Peace of 1763, the country enjoyed a long period of repose, and Sir John settled with his family at Balnagown Castle.

By his marriage, Sir John had issue—(1) Charles, his heir, (2) James, who became a Captain in the Royal Navy, and married in 1799 Catherine, only surviving daughter of James Farquharson of Invercauld; (3) George, an Advocate, and Judge of the Consistorial Court in Scotland; (4) John, who became a Colonel in the Coldstream Guards, and was killed at Talavera in 1809; (5) Robert, a Colonel in the Dragoon Guards. Sir John was succeeded by his eldest son,

VII., Sir Charles Ross, who was a Lieutenant-General in the Army, and Colonel of the 86th Regiment of Foot. He was twice married—(1) to Matilda Theresa, a Countess of the Roman Empire, and (2) to Lady Mary Fitzgerald, eldest daughter of William Robert, 2nd Duke of Leinster. By his marriage he had issue-(1) John, who died young; (2) Matilda, who married Admiral Sir Thomas Cochrane. She succeeded to the estate of her ancestor, Sir George Wishart of Oldiston, and took the surname of Wishart. By the second marriage there were born—(3) John Lockhart, who died unmarried; (4) Charles William

Augustus, who became the 8th Baronet; (5) Elizabeth, who died young; (6) Emilia Oliva, who married in 1819, Sir C.M. Lockhart, 2nd Baronet of Lee; (7) Mary, married in 1824 to Sir William Foulis, 8th Baronet of Ingleby; (8) and (9) Louisa and Geraldine, who remained unmarried.

VIII., Sir Charles William Augustus succeeded his father as 8th Baronet when he was only two years of age. He lived an uneventful life, taking comparatively little interest in public affairs. Eccentric in his habits, his chief pleasure lay in hunting, He was twice married—(1) to Elizabeth Baillie, eldest daughter of Colonel Robert Ross, 4th Dragoon Guards, fifth son of Sir John Lockhart Ross, Bart., who died without issue in 1848. Sir Charles married, secondly, in March 1865, Rebecca Sophia, third surviving daughter of Henry Barnes, Esq., of Tufnel Park, and had issue a son.

The following, which appeared in an Inverness newspaper, at the time of his death, is from the pen of his wife, Sophia, Lady Ross:—"Sir Charles was born on the 12th January, 1812, and succeeded his father as eighth Baronet on 8th February, 1814. He married (1) on the 9th February, 1841, his cousin, Elizabeth Baillie, eldest daughter of Colonel Robert Ross of the 4th Dragoon Guards, who died in 1843 without issue; (2) on 2nd March, 1865, Rebecca Sophia, third surviving daughter of Henry Barnes, Esq., of Tufnel Park, by whom he has a son, Charles Henry Augustus Frederick, born 4th April, 1872, who now succeeds to the estates and title. Lady Ross possesses considerable literary talent, and is known as the author of several well-known books. The estates are very valuable and extensive, being situated in the counties of Ross, Sutherland, and Lanark. In Ross-shire the family possessions are located in no less than seven parishes, viz., Fearn, Nigg, Logie, Kilmuir-Easter, Tain, Edderton, and Kincardine— the gross rental of which is at present over £15,000. The annual value of the estates in Sutherlandshire exeeds £1800, while that of the estate of Bonnington, in Lanarkshire, exeeds £1700, making together £18,500. Sir Charles was a Deputy-Lieutenant for Ross-shire and a Justice of the Peace for that county as well as for Cromarty and Lanarkshire. The Rosses of Balnagown are descended in the male line from the ancient Lanarkshire family of Lockhart of Lee.

The founder of the Balnagown family was William Lockhart, Esq., of Lockhart Hall, who was created a Baronet of Nova Scotia 28th February, 1668. Admiral Sir John Lockhart, a gallant and highly distinguished Naval officer, upon succeeding to the fortunes of his maternal uncle, General Ross, <u>assumed</u> the additional surname of <u>Ross</u>, and the estate of Lockhart being sold in 1762 adopted the designation of Balnagown. Sir John was born 11th November, 1721, and married Elizabeth, sole heiress of Lamington, daughter (by his first wife Henrietta, daughter and heiress of Sir James Carmichael of Bonnington) of Robert Dundas of Arniston, Lord President of the Court of Session. By this marriage the gallant Admiral's possessions were considerably increased. On his death he was succeeded by his eldest son, Sir Charles a Lieutenant-General in the Army, and Colonel of the 68th Regiment of Foot. who married (1), in 1788, Matilda Theresa, a Countess of Holy Roman Empire, being daughter and heiress of General Count James Lockhart of Carnwarth, by whom he had a son, who died in 1797, and a daughter who married the famous Admiral Sir Thomas Cochrane; (2), 15th June, 1799, Lady Mary Fitzgerald, eldest daughter of William Robert, 2nd Duke of Leinster, by whom he had issue two sons, of whom the subject of this notice the younger (the elder brother died, unmarried), and five daughters— two of whom married, namely, Emilia-Oliva, in 1819, to her cousin, Sir C.M. Lockhart of Lee, and Mary, in 1824, to Sir William Foulis, Bart., of Ingelby Manor.

The late Sir Charles was during his long life resident for the greater portion of each year upon his own estates. Ross-shire he regarded as his County, and in it he principally resided, and wherein he spent his income acting, in this respect, in marked contrast to many Scottish proprietors, who too frequently spend less time in their own counties, and less money on their own estates, than they do elsewhere. Sir Charles was an excellent sportsman, a very good angler, and a capital shot. He was particularly fond of grouse shooting, and within the last few years kept, for his own and his friends' amusement, a large moor in his own hands. He always appeared delighted at the approach of the shooting season when his period of migration to the hills he loved so well came round, Sir Charles was well-known for his kindness of heart and attachment to his tenants and dependants. Those who were constantly about him, and had, therefore, opportunities of knowing him best, will miss him most."

IX., Sir Charles Henry Augustus Frederick Lockhart, 9th Baronet, created in 1672. He is a Deputy-Lieutenant of the County of Ross. He was born 4th April, 1872, succeeded his father in 1883, married, first, in 1893, Winifred (4th in descent from the 7th Earl of Galloway and sister of Oliva, Countess Cairns), daughter of A.A. Berens, Esq. This marriage was dissolved in 1897. He married, secondly, Patricia Burnley, daughter of Andrew Ellison, of Louisville, U.S.A. He was educated at Eton and Trinity College, Cambridge. He rowed in the University Eight in 1894. A Lieutenant, 3rd Battalion Seaforth Highlanders, he retired in 1894. He served as Captain in Boer War, 1899-1900.

Sir Charles Ross has made a name for himself on two Continents by his "Ross Rifle," which is the national weapon of Canada and as a military and sporting weapon holds a high place. Sir Charles has made mechanics his hobby since his earliest years, and at Balnagown he had a "workshop" which was equipped with the latest appliances for work in metal and wood. He is not only expert in the use of tools, but has the inventive faculty, and this led him to his experiments for the improvement of the army and sporting rifles as they existed before the date of the last South African War. At that time the Canadian Government felt that something should be done to establish on Canadian soil a factory for the manufacture of small arms and ammunition. The Birmingham Small Arms Company were approached, but neither they nor any other British firm could be induced to lay down plant in Canada. It was then that Sir Charles Ross volunteered to establish a factory if the Government guaranteed the purchase of a sufficient number of rifles to justify the venture. Sir Charles submitted a rifle—with his own improvements—for acceptance, and after extensive tests and various further improvements which Sir Charles carried out, the factory was started and work begun, with an output of rifles that ultimately rose to a high figure annually.

Sir Charles took out his first patent for his rifle in 1893, and the list of subsequent patents makes up a formidable document. The rifle consists of about one hundred parts. and the later model—a sporting rifle— is considered by many users as a remarkably effective weapon. It is lighter than the military rifle, and its chief features are its great penetrating power, accuracy, absence of recoil, and its rapid-fire mechanism. These also are features of the army model. The rifles are manufactured in the factory of Quebec, and in an article on "Our National Arm," which appeared in the "Canadian Magazine" for September, 1908, it was stated that a contract for 100,000 rifles was then in hand from the British Government, and these had to be turned out within twelve months. These were completed within the specified time, in addition to the supplies required by the Canadian Government—which will give an idea of the extent of the Quebec factory.

Sir Charles Lockhart-Ross died without heirs. With his death the succession of the house of Lockhart-Ross of Balnagown, came to an end, also the Baronetcy of Nova Scotia. The property of Balnagown Castle was later sold and is presently owned by Mohamid Al Fayer, the store owner, Harrods of Knightsbridge, who occassionally comes here for hunting.

Authors note -
At Clan Gatherings one hears references made to Ross Rifle, the inventor of same being Sir Charles Lockhart-Ross, who assumed the name of Ross - the present day Clan Ross should not be that interested in this item.

Upon the death of Sir Charles Lockhart-Ross the Rosses of Pitcalnie, who were the true descendants of the Earls of Ross, presented their claim and Miss. Ethel Francis Sara Williamson Ross became Chief of the Clan.

The Lockhart-Rosses who owned and occupied Balnagowan Castle had assumed the name Ross and were never Chief of the Clan Ross. The Chiefship had been dormant during their tenure at Balnagowan from 1711 to 1903. The Pitcalnie Rosses were successful with their claim and Ethel Williamson Ross was elected Chief in 1903. She died in 1957 and her Sister Rosa Williamson Ross succeeded her as Chief of the Clan. Upon her death in 1968, being the last of her line, the Chiefship was transferred to the House of Shandwick, Sheriff Charles Campbell Ross was in line to become Chief but unfortunately did not survive her. The Chiefship passed to his son, David Campbell Ross, who is the present Chief of Clan Ross.

The Shandwick Rosses trace their line to the original Earls of Ross extending back to 1160's. The Chiefship had been dormant for nearly two hundred years, due to the manipulations of the Lockhart Rosses, it is indeed stiring times for the Clan Ross to have a true Chief of the blood.

Hail Ross

The late Chief Rosa R. Williamson Ross

The late Sheriff Campbell Ross Q.C., right with son, David Campbell Ross Chief of Clan and grandson.

David Ross of Ross
CHIEF OF CLAN ROSS

PERSONAL STANDARD
OF DAVID ROSS OF ROSS

MOTTO
Spem successus alit
Success nourishes hope

"Cadet Branches of Clan Ross"

The Rosses of Pitcalnie.

The Rosses of Kindeace.

The Rosses of Invercharron.

The Rosses of Braelangwall, Ankerville & Easter Fearn.

The Rosses of Tolly and Achnacloich.

The Rosses of Shandwick.

The Rosses of Aldie.

The Rosses of Balblair.

The Rosses of Pitkerry & Cromarty.

Septs of Clan Ross

ANDERSON Son of Andrew, The Gaelic name of the Clan Ross is 'Siol Aindrea' of 'Clann Aindrea' meaning 'race of Andrew' and the names are thus probably from the same progenitor. David le fiz Andrew of Pebbles and Duncan fiz Andrew of Dumfries took the oath in 1296. 'Anderson's Pill' made in the Lawnmarket, Edinburgh for over 20 years were a famous remedy, Jhon Anderson lived in Stobo in 1529.

ANDREWS From the names Andrew, Greek 'Aindrea' meaning manly. A popular first name because of Scotland's patron saint. The Andrews are a sept of Clan Ross and stem from the same progenitors. Duncan fiz Andrew gave homage in Dumfries in 1296. In Aberdeen in 1399 Wielelmus and Johann Andro were councillors.

CORBETT, CORBET From the French 'corbeau' a raven, Some Corbets settled in Ross and became affiliated with the Ross clan. Robert Corbet was a witness in 1124 in Selkirk. Donald Corbett held lands from John of Yle, earl of Ross in 1463. Many Corbets settled in Teviotdale in the early 12th century.

CROWE, CROW, CROY Possibly from Croy, Inverness-shire. John and Thomas Crow lived in Dunblane in 1470. James Crow (1800-1859) helped improve the ways of distilling whisky. Johanne Croy followed Walter Ross of Morange in 1596 (Inveravon).

DINGWALL From Dingwall in Ross. In 1342 John Younger of Dingwall witnessed a charter by William, Earl of Ross. There was once a Dingwall castle in Edinburgh. William of Dyngwale was dean of Aberdeen and Ross in 1389.

DUTHIE From the Gaelic 'Mac Gille Dubhthaigh' son of the servant of Dubhthach. The name may come from Saint Dubhthach of Tain, the Gaelic name of Tain being Baile Dhubhthaich. Marjory Duthe had a leasehold in Holm, Orkney.

GAIR, GEAR From the Gaelic 'gearr' short. MacIain Ghiorr in song and story was a reiver and pirate. Alexander Gar was a witness in Dornoch in 1535. The name still exists in Ross.

HAGGART This name is a corruption of MacTaggart and as such is descended from an early progenitor of the Clan Ross. There was a John Haggart in Perth in 1595.

MACANDREW Son of Andrew. From same progenitor of Clan Ross. See Anderson. Donald MaKandro was a victim of the plundering of Petty in 1502.

MACCULLOCH An old Galwegian name possibly from Gaelic 'MacCullaich' son of the boar. Thomas Maculagh of Wigton gave homage in 1296. Lulach was the name of the King who succeeded MacBeth. The MacCullochs held much land in the earldom of Ross and was a very respected name in that kingdom.

MACTAGGART, MACTAGGERT From the Gaelic 'Mac an t sagairt' son of the priest. Ferchar Machentagar of Mackinsagart was Earl of Ross in 1215. Catherine M'Target was accused of witchcraft in Dunbar in 1688. The MacTaggarts derive their origin from an early progenitor of Clan Ross.

MACTEAR, MACTEIR, MACTIER Short form of MacIntyre from the Gaelic 'Mac an t saoir' son of carpenter or wright. Paul MacTire was cousin of William, last Earl of Ross and when William died Paul MacTire became chief of the clan. Mactyr was a priest in Iona in 1372. In 1602 Catherine M'Teir was accused of witchcraft in Dundonald, Ayrshire (4 ml NE of Troon).

TULLOCH, TULLO, TULLOH From Tulloch in Dingwall. Nicholas de Tolach was a witness in 1364 in Brechin. Territorial connection to Clan Ross. Hector de Tulloch was canon in Orkney in 1467.

VASS, VAUS, WAUS, WASS From 'Vaux' French name meaning dales. Of English origin, a branch settled in Dirleton, East Lothian in the 12th century. John de

Vallibus was witness to a grant in Ednam in 1174. The name is a sept of Clan Ross and the Vasses often fought under Clan Ross.

Balnagowan Castle

SCOTTISH
CREST BADGES

THE COURT OF THE LORD LYON
H.M. NEW REGISTER HOUSE
EDINBURGH, EH1 3YT. TEL. 031-556-7255

INTRODUCTION

Much confusion exists about the meaning, use and entitlement to wear Scottish Crest Badges, and it is constantly increased by well-meaning but ill-informed explanations. This leaflet is authoritative in setting out the main facts.

Even the popular name "Clan Crest" is a misnomer, as there is no such thing as a "Clan" Crest. The Crest is the exclusively **personal** property of the Clan Chief, and it is fully protected to him by the law in Scotland. The circumstances in which it may be worn by his clansmen are set out hereinafter.

CLANSMEN AND CLANSWOMEN

I.E. The Chief's relatives, including his own immediate family and even his eldest son, and ALL members of the extended family called the "Clan", whether bearing the Clan surname or that of one of its septs; **in sum**, all those who profess allegiance to that Chief and wish to demonstrate their association with the clan.

It is correct for these to wear their Chief's Crest encircled with a STRAP AND BUCKLE bearing their Chief's Motto or Slogan. The strap and buckle is the sign of the clansman, and he demonstrates his membership of his Chief's Clan by wearing his Chief's Crest within it.

Although the Crest Badge is purchased by and is therefore owned by the clansman, the heraldic Crest and Motto on it belong to the Chief and **NOT** to the clansman. They are the Chief's exclusive heraldic property, which the clansman is only thus permitted to wear.

It is illegal for the clansman to misappropriate the Chief's Crest and Motto for any other use of his own, such as decorating his own silver, writing paper or signet ring, which anyway would mean that these articles belonged to the Chief who is the owner of the Crest and Motto on them.

Clan Societies, Officials and clansmen who have reason to use the Crest Badge on stationery should add beneath it the words "Crest Badge of a member of the Clan...", to make it clear that the Crest Badge is not being misappropriated by the Clan Society or Official involved. It is the Crest Badge of ALL clansmen, whether members of Clan Societies or not, and non-members may not be excluded if they are clansmen.

THE HIGHLAND CLEARANCES

CHAPTER 3

"Lochaber No More" — from an engraving by Charles Couseu after a painting by J Watson Nicol.
(Courtesy BBC Hulton Picture Library)

LIVINGSTONE'S
CALEDONIAN CRITIC.

"LET YOUR MASTERS COME AND ATTACK US, WE ARE READY TO MEET THEM."—
SIR WILLIAM WALLACE

No. 1.] FEBRUARY, 1852. [Price 3D.

PROSPECTUS

In presenting these pages to the public, we have only to intimate—1st. That a shameful and criminal neglect of truthfully representing the national character prevailed to a lamentable extent, for the last century at least. That the origin of that evil had its rise among a class of designing men, who transmitted the said rancorous animosity to their posterity to the present day. That from the same source emanated that sweeping flood of oppression, defamation, vice, ignorance, and undisguised Heathenism, which now prevail to so alarming an extent, that there is little hope of National Reform. Nevertheless, it is a Christian duty, binding upon every Scot, who have the least spark of Christian principle—binding upon every man in this kingdom, who can claim Caledonia for their mother, to unite, and come boldly out to develope her national character, in all its bearings—to develope her vast literary resources, buried by her enemies, many of which are among her own ungrateful sons, to develope the fact, that she is indeed the first of the European nations who set bounds to the highest political power that ever existed; and that she is the last of the Euro-

" THE HIGHLAND CLEARANCES "

In these pages the full horrifying story of the Highland Clearances unfolds.

Man's inhumanity to man was brought sharply into focus in those grim days of the early nineteenth century when entire communities were swept away so that the land could be sold off to southern sheep farmers.

These were times of betrayal and bravery and of cruelty and deception.

There was betrayal of the people by the clan chiefs who, after the fiasco of the '45, had no need for heroic men to fight their wars. Power now lay in money relised from the sale of land — not in land won and kept in battle by loyal men who gave their blood for the soil.

Even the clergy betrayed their flocks who were largely illiterate but deeply religious and God fearing folk. Highlanders saw the minister as the stern oracle of the truth but, sadly, he was often the puppet of the estate whose power he feared and whose support he received. The theme from pulpit to pew was that troubles were merely part of the punishment inflicted by Providence in the course of man working out his redemption.

Bravery was the hallmark of the folk forced to leave these shores for the Americas and Australia. Conditions on the emigrant ships were horrific with travellers packed together like sardines regardless of comfort and the decencies of life and with insufficient food. Many died from disease and famine. Those who made it encountered sub zero or very high temperatures to which they couldn't adjust. In America many were abandoned and massacred by Red Indians. Others had to tramp for weeks through trackless forests to Upper Canada where there were settlements of fellow Scots who could provide food and shelter.

Through time, though, hundreds of these emigrants prospered and lived to enjoy a good life in the New World. Back home things, ironically, turned full cycle and some of their worst oppressors fell on hard times.

The cruelty displayed by the evicting mobs is vividly described from eye-witness accounts taken at the time. Even the old sick and infirm were tossed out into the heather and their homes pulled down around their ears. Many tenants died from alarm, fatigue and cold. Those who lived attempted to build makeshift homes from old bits of wood and trees but always the laird's men would come and demolish even these humble efforts. One family tried to find shelter living in a graveyard but even that was not permitted.

There was deception of the people at home and abroad by the estate owners and their factors. Clearances were necessary to make better use of the land as sheep would contribute more to the well being of the country generally than crofters and cows it was argued. Displaced families could make a good living on the coast and from the sea. Nobody was forced to emigrate. But in reality hundreds ended up living on rocky land along the water's edge and their only food was cockles picked from the shore supplemented by mixing cattle blood with oatmeal which was cut into slices and fried. And, all too often, entire families were taken from their homes and put on ships for distant lands on the other side of the world.

    Most of the material was written by Alexander Mackenzie and first published in 1883. The selection of stories and experiences featured here is taken from the 1914 edition produced by E. Mackay of Stirling.

    An introduction to this later edition refers to Mr Mackenzie as a Highlander "who commanded in a great measure the esteem of fellow Highlanders and collected for the first time the sane and authenticated accounts of the experiences of the people in the great agrarian crisis of their history.

    "The Highlander loves his past and the story of the great wrongs of the days of the clearances is still deeply embedded in his days".

    The great Sir Walter Scott, who made frequent attacks on the activities of the big landowners, wrote: " The Highlands have been drained of a whole mass of inhabitants, dispossessed by an unrelenting avarice, which will one day be found to have been as short sighted as it is unjust and selfish".

    All chapters are by Alexander Mackenzie unless otherwise stated. Copy has been shortened or rewritten in certain passages for ease of reading.

Angry women battle Sheriff's men—

The constitution of society in the Glen, says Mr Robertson, is remarkably simple. Four heads of families are bound for the whole rental.

The number of souls was about ninety, sixteen cottages paid rent; they supported a teacher for the education of their own children; they supported their own poor.

"The laird has never lost a farthing of rent in bad years, such as 1836 and 1837, the people may have required the favour of a few weeks' delay, but they are not now a single farthing in arrears;" that is, when they are in receipt of summonses of removal.

"For a century", Mr Robertson continues, speaking of the Highlanders, "their privileges have been lessening; they dare not now hunt the deer, or shoot the grouse or the blackcock; they have no longer the range of the hills for their cattle and their sheep; they must not catch a salmon in the stream; in earth, air, and water, the rights of the laird are greater, and the rights of the people are smaller, than they were in the days of their forefathers".

The same writer eloquently concludes:—

"The father of the laird of Kindeace bought Glencalvie. It was sold by a Ross two short centuries ago. The swords of the Rosses of Glencalvie did their part in protecting this little glen, as well as the broad lands of Pitcalvie, from the ravages and clutches of hostile septs.

These clansmen bled and died in the belief that every principle of honour and morals secured their descendants a right to subsisting on the soil.

The chiefs and their children had the same charter of the sword.

Some Legislatures have made the right of the people superior to the right of the chief; British law-makers made the rights of the chief everything, and those of their followers nothing.

The ideas of the morality of property are in most men the creatures of their interests and sympathies.

Others state that they not only did their duty, but that less firmness might have provided fatal to themselves.

The instances of violence are certainly, though very

naturally, on the part of the attacking force; several batons were smashed in the melee; a great number of men and women were seriously hurt, especially about the head and face, while not one of the policemen, so far as we can learn, suffered any injury in consequence.

As soon as the mob was fairly dispersed, the police made active pursuit, in the hope of catching some of the ringleaders.

The men had, however, fled, and the only persons apprehended were some women, who had been active in the opposition, and who had been wounded.

They were conveyed to the prison at Tain, but liberated on bail next day, through the intercession of a gallant friend, who became responsible for their appearance".

"A correspondent writes", continues the *Courier,* "ten young women were wounded in the back of the skull and other parts of their bodies...The wounds on these women show plainly the severe manner in which they were dealt with by the police when they were retreating.

It was currently reported last night that one of them was dead; and the feelings of indignation is so strong against the manner in which the constables have acted, that I fully believe the life of any stranger, if he were supposed to be an officer of the law, would not be worth twopence in the district".

Of this there cannot be a doubt, however, the chiefs would not have had the land at all, could the clansmen have foreseen the present state of the Highlands—their children in mournful groups going into exile — the faggot of legal myrmidons in the thatch of the feal cabin — the hearths of their homes and their lives in the green sheep-walks of the stranger.

Sad it is, that it is seemingly the will of our constituencies that our laws shall prefer the few to the many.

Most mournful will it be, should the clansmen of the Highlands have been cleared away, ejected, exiled, in deference to a political, a moral, a social, and an economical mistake — a suggestion not of philosophy, but of mammon — a system in which the demon of sordidness assumed the shape of the angel of civilization and light."

That the Eviction of the Rosses was of a harsh character is amply corroborated by the following account, extracted from the *Inverness Courier:*—

"At six o'clock on the morning of Friday last, Sheriff Taylor proceeded from Tain, accompanied by several Sheriff's officers, and a police force of about thirty.

On arriving at Greenyards, which is nearly four miles from Bonar Bridge, it was found that about three hundred persons, fully two-thirds of whom were women, had assembled from the county round about, all apparently prepared to resist execution of the law.

The women stood in front, armed with stones, and the men occupied the background, all, or nearly all, furnished with sticks.

The Sheriff attempted to reason with the crowd, and to show them the necessity of yielding to the law: but his efforts were fruitless; and he was reluctantly obliged to employ force.

After a sharp resistance, which happily lasted only a few minutes, the people were dispersed, and the Sheriff was enabled to execute the summonses upon the four tenants.

The women, as they bore the brunt of the battle, were the principal sufferers. A large number of them — fifteen of sixteen, we believe, were seriously hurt, and of these several are under medical treatment; one woman, we believe, still lies in a precarious condition..

The policemen appear to have used their batons with great force, but they escaped themselves almost unhurt.

Several correspondents from the district complain that the policemen used their batons with wanton cruelty.

CROICK CHURCH IN EASTER ROSS,

The names and dates scratched in the panes of a window of the church is evidence of another shocking story of the Clearances — when sheep were more valuable than people.

In 1842 James Gillianders, factor to Robertsons of Kindeace, evícted the tenants of Glencalvie in a most brutal manner, which left 90 people homeless, while the Factor burned the roofs from their homes. Having no place to go, many made makeshift lean-to tents in the Croick Church yard, where they remained for over a week. During their stay they scratched their names, dates and messages on the window glass of east window of the Church. They also recorded information about the evictions from Greenyards in Strathcarron, which is refered to as Massacre of Rosses in John Prebbles book "The Highland Clearances." These messages may still be seen today.

East window of Croick Church where evicted Rosses scratched messages on window glass.

'Incredible' journeys

Mr Robert Brown, Sheriff-Substitute of the Western District of Inverness-shire, in summing up the number who left from 1801 to 1803, says:—

"In the year 1801, a Mr George Dennon, from Pictou, carried out two cargoes of emigrants from Fort William to Pictou, consisting of about seven hundred souls.

A vessel sailed the same season from Isle Martin with about one hundred passengers, it is believed, from the same place.

No more vessels sailed that year; but in 1802, eleven large ships sailed with emigrants to America.

Of these, four were from Fort William, one from Knoydart, one from Isle Martin, one from Uist, one from Greenock.

Five of these were bound for Canada, four for Pictou, and one for Cape Breton.

The only remaining vessel, which took a cargo of people in Skye, sailed for Wilmington, in the United States.

In the year 1803, exclusive of Lord Selkirk's transport, eleven cargoes of emigrants went from the North Highlands.

Of these, four were from the Moray Firth, two from Ullapool, three from Stornoway, and two from Fort William.

The whole of these cargoes were bound for the British settlements, and most of them were discharged at Pictou".

Soon after, several other vessels sailed from the North West Highlands with emigrants, the whole of whom were for the British Colonies.

In addition to these, Lord Selkirk took out 250 from South Uist in 1802, and in 1803 he sent out to Prince Edward Island about 800 souls, in three different vessels, most of whom were from the Island of Skye, and the remainder from Ross-shire, North Argyll, the interior of the county of Inverness, and the Island of Uist.

In 1804, 1805, and 1806, several cargoes of Highlanders left Mull, Skye, and Western Islands, for Prince Edward

Island and other North American Colonies.

Altogether, not less than 10,000 souls left the Western Highlands and Islands during the first six years of the present century, a fact which will now appear incredible.

Sir Walter Scott wrote:—

"In too many instances the Highlands have been drained, not of their superfluity of population, but the whole mass of the inhabitants, dispossessed by an unrelenting avarice, which will be one day found to have been as short-sighted as it is unjust and selfish.

Meantime, the Highlands may become the fairy ground for romance and poetry, or the subject of experiment for the professors of speculation, political and economical.

But if the hour of need should come, and it may not, perhaps, be far distant — the pibrich may sound through the deserted region but the summons will remain unanswered."

Highland ox " Monarch of the Glen ".

Grass and earth were dyed red with blood

In a "Sermon for the Times", the Rev. Richard Hibbs of the Episcopal Church, Edinburgh, referring to these evictions, says:— "Take first, the awful proof how far in opression men can go — men highly educated and largely gifted in every way — property, talents, all; for the most part indeed, they are so-called noblemen.

What, then, are they doing in the Highland districts, according to the testimony of a learned professor in this city?

Why, depopulating those districts in order to make room for red deer. And how? By buying off the cottars, and giving them money to emigrate?

Not at all, but by starving them out; by rendering them absolutely incapable of procuring subsistence for themselves and families; for they first take away from them their apportionments of poor lands, although they may have paid their rents; and if that doesn't suffice to eradicate from their hearts that love of the soil on which they have been born and bred these inhuman landlords take away from the poor cottars the very roof above their defenceless heads, and expose them to the inclemencies of a northern sky; and this, forsooth, because they must have plenty room for their dogs and deer.

For plentiful instances of the most wanton barbarities under this head we need only point to the Knoydart evictions. Here were perpetrated such enormities as might well have caused the very sun to hide his face at noon-day".

The reader, utterly appalled by these horrifying statements, finds it difficult to retain the recollection that he is perusing the history of his own times, and country too.

He would fain yield himself to the tempting illusion that the ruthless astrocities which are depicted were enacted in a fabulous period, in ages long past; or some far distant, uncivilized region of our globe.

But alas! it is Scotland, in the latter half of the

nineteenth century, of which he reads.

One feature of the heart-harrowing case is the cruelty that was practised on this occasion upon the female portion of the evicted clan.

Mr D. Ross, in a letter addressed to the Right Hon. the Lord Advocate, Edinburgh, dated April 19, 1854, writes in reference to one of those clearances and evictions which had just then taken place, under the authority of a certain Sheriff of the district, and by means of a body of policemen as executioners:— " The feeling on this subject, not only in the district, but in Sutherlandshire and Ross-shire, is, among the great majority of the people, one of universal condemnation of the Sheriff's reckless conduct, and of indignation and disgust at the brutality of the policemen.
Such, indeed, was the sad havoc made on the females on the banks of the Carron, on the memorable 31st March last, that pools of blood were upon the ground — that the grass and earth were dyed red with it — that the dogs of the district came and licked up the blood; and at last, such was the state of feeling of parties who went from a distance to see the field, that a party (it is understood by order or instructions from headquarters) actually harrowed the ground during the night to hide the blood!

The affair at Greenyard, on the morning of the 31st March last, is not calculated to inspire much love of country, or rouse the martial spirit of the already ill-used Highlanders.

The savage treatment of innocent females on that morning, by an enraged body of police, throws the Sinope butchery into the shade; for the Ross-shire Haynaus have shown themselves more cruel and more blood-thirsty than the Austrian women-floggers.

What could these poor men and women — with their wounds and scars, and broken bones, and disjointed arms, stretched on beds of sickness, or moving on crutches, the result of the brutal treatment of them by the police at Greenyard — have to dread from the invasion of Scotland by Russia?"

Commenting on this incredible atrocity, committed in the middle of the nineteenth century, Donald Macleod says truly that:— "It was so horrifying and so brutal that he did not wonder at the rev. gentleman's delicacy in speaking of it, and directing his hearers to peruse Mr Ross's pamphlet for full information".

Mr Ross went from Glasgow to Greenyard to investigate the case upon the spot, and found that Mr Taylor, a native of Sutherland, well educated in the evicting schemes and murderous cruelty of that county, and Sheriff-substitute of Ross-shire, marched from Tain upon the morning of the 31st March, at the head of a strong party of armed constables, with heavy bludgeons and fire-arms, conveyed in carts and other vehicles. They were allowed as much drink as they chose to take so as to qualify them for the bloody work which they had to perform; fit for any outrage, fully equipped, and told by the Sheriff to show no mercy to any one who would oppose them,

In this excited, half-drunken state, they came in contact with the unfortunate women of Greenyard, who were determined to prevent the officers from serving the summonses of removal upon them, and keep the holding of small farms where they and their forefathers lived and died for generations.

But no time was allowed for parley; the Sheriff gave the order to clear the way, and, be it said to his everlasting disgrace, he struck the first blow at a woman, the mother of a large family, and large in the family way at the time, who tried to keep him back; then a general slaughter commenced; the women made noble resistance, until the bravest of them got their arms broken; then they gave way.

This did not allay the rage of the murderous brutes, they continued clubbing at the protectless creatures until every one of them was stretched on the field, weltering in their blood, or with broken arms, ribs, and bruised limbs.

In this woeful condition many of them were handcuffed together, others tied with coarse ropes, huddled into carts, and carried prisoners to Tain.

I have seen myself in the possession of Mr Ross, Glasgow, patches or scalps of the skin with the long hair adhering to them, which was found upon the field a few days after this inhuman affray.

I did not see the women, but I was told that gashes were found on the heads of two young female prisoners in

Tain jail, which exactly corresponded with the slices of scalps which I have seen, so that Sutherland and Ross-shire may boast of having had the Nana Sahib and his chiefs some few years before India.

Mr Donald Ross placed the whole affair before the Lord Advocate for Scotland, but no notice was taken of it by that functionary, further than that the majesty of the law would need to be observed and attended to.

From the same estate (the estate of Robertson of Kindeace, if I am not mistaken in the date) in the year 1843, the whole inhabitants of Glencalvie were evicted in a similar manner, and so unprovided and unprepared were they for removal at such an inclement season of the year, that they had to shelter themselves in a Church and a burying-ground.

I have seen myself nineteen families within this gloomy and solitary resting abode of the dead. They were there for months.

In the year 1819 or '20, about the time when the depopulation of Sutherland was completed, and the annual conflagration of burning the houses ceased, a sheep farmer from there fixed his eyes upon a glen in Ross-shire, inhabited by a brave, hardy race from time immemorial.

Summonses of removal were served upon them at once. The people resisted — a military force was brought against them — the military and the women of the glen met at the entrance to the glen, and a bloody conflict took place; without reading the riot act or taking any other precaution, the military fired (by the order of Sheriff MacLeod) ball cartridge upon the women; one young girl of the name of Mathieson was shot dead on the spot; many were wounded.

When this murder was observed by the survivors, and some young men concealed in the background, they made a heroic sudden rush upon the military, when a hand-to-hand melee or fight took place.

In a few minutes the military were put to disorder by flight; in their retreat they were unmercifully dealt with, only two of them escaping with whole heads.

The Sheriff's coach was smashed to atoms, and he made a narrow escape himself with a whole head.

But no legal cognizance was taken of this affair, as the

Sheriff and the military were the violators.

However, for fear of prosecution, the Sheriff settled a pension of £6 sterling yearly upon the murdered girl's father, and the case was hushed up likewise.

The result was that the people kept possession of the glen, and that the proprietor and the oldest and most insatiable of Sutherland scourges went to law, which ended in the ruination of the latter, who died a pauper".

Hugh Miller, describing a "Highland Clearing", in one of his able leading articles in the *Witness*, since published in volume form, quotes freely from an article by John Robertson, which appeared in the *Glasgow National* in August, 1844, on the evictions of the Rosses of Glencalvie.

When the article from which Hugh Miller quotes was written, the inhabitants of the glen had just received notices of removal, but the evictions had not yet been carried out.

Commenting on the proceedings Hugh Miller says:—

"In a adjacent glen (to Strathcarron) a summons of removal has been served within the last few months on a whole community."

Lots of deer forests in the Highlands.

In three years 5390 souls were driven from the glens

A chief's widow, *Marsali Bhinneach* — Marjory, daughter of Sir Ludovick Grant of Dalvey, widow of Duncan Macdonnell of Glengarry, who died in 1788 — gave the whole of Glencruaich as a sheep farm to one south country shepherd, and to make room for him she evicted over 500 people from their ancient homes.

The bad example of this heartless woman was unfortunately imitated-afterwards by her daughter Elizabeth, who, in 1801, cleared Strathglass almost to a man of its inhabitants.

No less than 799 took ship at Fort William and Isle Martin from Strathglass, the Aird, Glen Urquhart, and the neighbouring districts, all for Pictou, Nova Scotia; while in the following year, 473 from the same district left Fort William, for Upper Canada, and 128 for Pictou.

Five hundred and fifty went aboard another ship at Knoydart, many of whom were from Strathglass.

In 1803, four different batches of 120 souls each, by four different ships, left Strathglass, also for Pictou; while not a few went away with emigrants from other parts of the Highlands.

During these three years we find that no less than 5390 were driven out of these Highland glens, and it will be seen that a very large proportion of them were evicted from Strathglass by the daughter of the notorious *Marsali Bhinneach*.

From among the living cargo of one of the vessels which sailed from Fort William no less than fifty-three souls died, on the way out, of an epidemic; and, on the arrival of the living portion of the cargo at Pictou, they were shut in on a narrow point of land, from whence they were not allowed to communicate with any of their friends who had gone before them, for fear of communicating the contagion, Here they suffered indescribable hardships.

Voyage of despair

The reader is already acquainted with the misery endured by those evicted from Barra and South Uist by Colonel Gordon, after their arrival in Canada. This was no isolated case.

We shall here give a few instances of the unspeakable suffering of those pioneers who left so early as 1773, in the ship *Hector,* for Pictou, Nova Scotia.

The *Hector* was owned by two men, Pagan and Witherspoon who bought three shares of land in Pictou, and they engaged a Mr John Ross as their agent, to accompany the vessel to Scotland, to bring out as many colonists as could be induced, by misrepresentation and falsehoods, to leave their homes.

They offered a free passage, a farm, and a year's free provisions to their dupes.

On his arrival in Scotland, Ross drew a glowing picture of the land and other manifold advantages of the country to which he was enticing the people.

The highlanders knew nothing of the difficulties awaiting them in a land covered over with a dense unbroken forest.

Calling first at Greenock, three families and five single young men joined the vessel at that port.

She then sailed to Lochbroom in Ross-shire, where she received 33 families and 25 single men, the whole of her passengers numbering about 200 souls.

This band, in the beginning of July, 1773, bade a final farewell to their native land, not a soul on board having ever crossed the Atlantic except a single sailor and John Ross, the agent.

As they were leaving, a piper came on board who had not paid his passage; the captain ordered him ashore, but the strains of the national instrument affected those on board so much that they pleaded to have him allowed to accompany them, and offered to share their own rations with him in exchange for his music during the passage.

Their request was granted, and his performance aided in no small degree to cheer the noble band of pioneers in their long voyage of eleven weeks, in a miserable hulk, across the Atlantic.

The pilgrim band kept up their spirits as best they could by song, pipe music, dancing, wrestling, and other amusements, through the long and painful voyage.

The ship was so rotten that the passengers could pick the wood out of her sides with their fingers.

They met with a severe gale off the Newfoundland coast, and were driven back by it so far that it took them about fourteen days to get back to the point at which the storm met them.

The accommodation was wretched, smallpox and dysentery broke out among the passengers.

Eighteen of the children died, and were committed to the deep amidst such anguish and heart-rending agony as only a Highlander can understand.

Their stock of provisions became almost exhausted, the water became scarce and bad; the remnants of provision left consisted mainly of salt meat, which, from the scarcity of water, added greatly to their sufferings.

The oatcake carried by them became mouldy, so that much of it had been thrown away before they dreamt of having such a long passage.

Fortunately for them, one of the passengers, Hugh Macleod, more prudent than the others, gathered up the despised scraps into a bag, and during the last few days of the voyage his fellows were too glad to join him in devouring this refuse to keep souls and bodies together.

At last the *Hector* dropped anchor in the harbour, opposite where the town of Pictou now stands.

Though the Highland dress was then proscribed at home, this emigrant band carried theirs along with them, and, in celebration of their arrival, many of the younger men donned their national dress — to which a few of them were able to add the *Sgian Dubh* and the Claymore — while the piper blew up his pipes with might and main, its thrilling tones, for the first time, startling the denizens of the endless forest, and its echoes resounding through the wild solitude.

Scottish emigrants are admitted upon all hands to have given its backbone of moral and religious strength to the Province, and to those brought over from the Highlands in this vessel is due the honour of being in the forefront — the pioneers and vanguard.

But how different was the reality to the expectations of these poor creatures, led by the plausibility of the emigration agent, to expect free estates on their arrival.

The whole scene, as far as the eye could see, was a dense forest.

They crowded on the deck to take stock of their future home, and their hearts sank within them.

They were landed without the provisions promised, without shelter of any king, and were only able, by the aid of those few before them, to erect camps of the rudest and most primitive description, to shelter their wives and their children from the elements.

Their feelings of disappointment were most bitter.

Many of them sat down in the forest and wept bitterly hardly any provisions were possessed leaving them almost destitute.

It was now too late to raise any crops that year.

To make matters worse, they were sent some three miles into the forest, so that they could not even take advantage with the same ease of any fish that might be caught in the harbour.

The whole thing appeared an utter mockery.

To unskilled men the work of clearing seemed hopeless; they were naturally afraid of the Red Indian and of the wild beasts of the forest; without roads or paths, they were frightened to move for fear of getting lost.

It would be tedious to describe the sufferings which they afterwards endured. Many of them left.

Others, fathers, mothers, and children, bound themselves away, as virtual slaves, in other settlements, for mere subsistence.

TENANTS PERIOD COTTAGE

Those who remained lived in small huts, covered only with the bark of branches of trees to shelter them from the bitter winter cold.

They had to walk some eighty miles, through a trackless forest, in deep snow to Truro, to obtain a few bushels of potatoes, or a little flour in exchange for their labour, dragging these back all the way again on their backs, and endless cases of great suffering from actual want occured.

In the following spring they set to work. They cleared some of the forest, and planted a larger crop.

They learned to hunt the moose, a kind of large deer.

They began to cut timber, and sent a cargo of it from Pictou — the first of a trade very profitabley and extensively carried on ever since.

The population had; however, grown less than it was before their arrival; for in this year it amounted to only 78 persons.

One of the modes of laying up a supply of food for the winter was to dig up a large quantity of clams or large oysters, pile them in large heaps on the sea-shore, and then cover them over with sand, though they were often, in winter, obliged to cut through ice more than a foot thick to get to them.

This will give a fair idea of the hardships experienced by the earlier emigrants in these colonies.

In Prince Edward Island, however, a colony from Lockerbie, in Dumfriesshire, who came out in 1774, seemed to have fared even worse.

They began operations on the island with fair prospects of success, when a plague of locusts, or field mice, broke out, and consumed everything, even the potatoes in the ground; and for eighteen months the settlers experienced all the miseries of a famine, having for several months only what lobsters or shell-fish they could gather from the sea-shore.

The winter brought them to such a state of weakness that they were unable to convey food a reasonable distance even when they had means to buy it.

Who can think of these early hardships and cruel existences without condemning — even hating — the memories of the harsh and heartless Highland and Scottish lairds, who made existance at home even almost as miserable for those noble fellows, and who then drove them in thousands out of their native land, not caring one iota whether they sank in the Atlantic, or were starved to death on a strange and uncongenial soil?

Retributive justice demands that posterity should execrate the memories of the authors of such misery and horrid cruelty.

It may seem uncharitable to write thus of the dead; but it is impossible to forget their inhuman conduct, though, no thanks to them, it has turned out for the better, for the descendants of those who were banished to what was then infinitely worse than transportation for the worst crimes. Such criminals were looked after and cared for; but those poor fellows, driven out of their homes by the Highland lairds, and sent across there, were left to starve, helpless, and uncared for.

Many died from deadly fever on emigrant ship

His lordship's position in regard to the proceedings was most unfortunate.

Donald Ross, writing as an eye-witness of these evictions, says —

"Some years ago Lord Macdonald incurred debts on his property to the extent of £200,000 sterling, and his lands being entailed, his creditors could not dispose of them, but they placed a trustee over them in order to intercept certain portions of the rent in payment of the debt.

Lord Macdonald, of course, continues to have an interest and a surveillance over the property in the matter of removals, the letting of the fishings and shootings, and the general improvement of his estates.

The trustee and the local factor under him have no particular interest in the property, nor in the people thereon, beyond collecting their quota of the rents for the creditors; consequently the property is mismanaged, and the crofter and cottar population are greatly neglected.

The tenants of SUISINISH and BORERAIG were the descendants of a long line of peasantry on the Macdonald estates, and were remarkable for their patience, loyalty, and general good conduct."

The only plea made at the time of evicting them was that of over-population.

Ten families received the usual summonses, and passages were secured for them in the *Hercules,* an unfortunate ship which sailed with a cargo of passengers under the auspices of a body calling itself "The Highland and Island Emigration Society".

A deadly fever broke out among the passengers, the ship was detained at Cork in consequence, and a large number of the passengers died of the epidemic.

After the sad fate of so many of those previously cleared out, in the ill-fated ship, it was generally thought that some compassion would be shown for those who had been still permitted to remain.

Not so, however. On the 4th of April 1853, they were all

warned out of their holdings.

They petitioned and pleaded with his lordship to no purpose.

They were ordered to remove their cattle from the pasture, and themselves from their houses and lands.

Subsequently, however, they were informed that they would get land on another part of the estate — portions of a barren moor, quite unfit for cultivation.

In the middle of September of following, Lord Macdonald's ground officer, with a body of constables, arrived, and at once proceeded to eject in the most heartless manner the whole population, numbering 32 families, and that at a period when the able-bodied male members of the families were away from home trying to earn something by which to pay their rents, and help to carry their families through the coming winter.

In spite of the wailing of the helpless women and children, the cruel work was proceeded with as rapidly as possible, and without the slightest apparent compunction.

"The scene was truly heart-rending. The women and children went about tearing their hair, and rending the heavens with their cries.

Mothers with tender infants at the breast looked helplessly on, while their effects and their aged and infirm relatives, were cast out, and the doors of their houses locked in thier faces."

The young children, poor, helpless, little creatures, gathered in groups, and gave vent to their feelings in loud and bitter wailings.

"No mercy was shown to age or sex, all were indiscriminately thrust out and left to perish on the hills."

Untold cruelties were perpetrated on this occasion to the helpless creatures during the absence of their husbands and other principal breadwinners.

Donald Ross in his pamphlet, "Real Scottish Grievances", published in 1854, and who not only was an eye-witness, but generously supplied the people with a great quantity of food and clothing, describes several of the cases. I can only find room here, however, for his first.

Flora Robertson or Matheson, a widow, aged 96 years, was then residing with her son, Alexander Matheson, who had a small lot of land in Suisinish.

Her son was a widower, with four children; and shortly before the time for evicting the people arrived, he went to labour at harvest in the south, taking his oldest boy with him.

The grandmother and the three other children were left in the house.

"When the evicting officers and factor arrived, the poor old woman was sitting on a coach outside the house.

The day being fine, her grandchildren lifted her out of bed and brought her to the door.

She was very frail; and it would have gladdened any heart to see how the two youngest of her grandchildren helped her along; how they seated her where there was most shelter; and then, how they brought her some clothing and clad her, and endeavoured to make her comfortable.

The gratitude of the old woman was unbounded in these little acts of kindness and compassion; and the poor children, on the other hand, felt highly pleased at finding their services so well appreciated.

Nothing could exceed the beauty of the scene. The sea was glittering with millions of little waves and globules, and looked like a lake of silver, gently agitated.

The hills, with the heather in full bloom, and with the wild flowers in their beauty, had assumed all the colours of the rainbow, and were most pleasant to the eye to look upon.

The crops of corn in the neighbourhood were beginning to get yellow for the harvest; the small patches of potatoes were under flower, and promised well; the sheep and the cattle, as if tired of feeding, had lain down to rest on the face of the hills; and the dogs, as if satisfied their services were not required for a time, chose for themselves pleasant, well-sheltered spots and lay basking at full length in the sun.

Even the little boats on the loch, though their sails were spread, made no progress, but lay at rest, reflecting their own tiny shadows on the bosom of the deep, still waters.

The scene was most enchanting; and, although old Flora's eyes were getting dim with age, she looked on the objects before her with great delight.

While the old woman was thus enjoying the benefit of the fresh air, admiring the beauty of the landscape, and just when the poor children had entered the house to prepare a frugal meal for themselves and their aged charge, a sudden barking of dogs gave signal intimation of the approach of strangers.

The native inquisitiveness of the young ones was immediately set on edge, and off they set across the fields, and over the fences, after the dogs.

They soon returned, however, with horror depicted on their countenances; they had a fearful tale to unfold.

The furniture and other effects of their nearest neighbours, just across the hill, they saw thrown out; they heard the children screaming, and they saw the factor's men putting bars and locks on the doors.

This was enough. The heart of the old woman, so recently revived and invigorated, was now set to break within her.

What was she to do? What could she do?

Absolutely nothing!

The poor children thought that if they could only get their aged granny inside before the evicting officers arrived then all would be well.

The officers, however, arrived before they could get this accomplished; and instead of letting the old woman in, they threw out before the door every article that was inside the house, and then they placed large bars and padlocks on the door!

The grandchildren were horror-struck at this procedure — and no wonder.

Here the were, shut out of the house and home, their father and elder brother several hundred miles away from them, and their mother dead. The only shelter was a sheep cot a few hundred yards away and with some difficulty they dragged their gran there.

It was a most wretched habitation, quite unfit for human beings, yet here the widow was compelled to remain until the following December.

When her son came home from the harvest in the south, he was amazed at the treatment his aged mother and his children had received.

He was then in good health; but a few weeks in the cold and damp of the sheep cot had a most deadly effect upon his health, for he was seized with violent cramps, then with a cough; at last his limbs and body swelled, and then he died!

When dead, his corpse lay across the floor, his feet at the opposite wall, and his head being at the door, the wind waved his long black hair to and fro until he was placed in his coffin.

The inspector of the poor, who was also ground officer to Lord Macdonald, and chief officer in the evictions, at last appeared, and removed the old woman to another house; not, however, until he was threatened with prosecution for neglect of duty.

The grandchildren were also removed from the sheep cot, for they were ill; Peggy and William were seriously so, but Sandy, although ill, could walk a little.

The inspector for the poor gave the children, during their illness, only 14 lbs. of meal and 3 lbs. of rice, as aliment for three weeks, and nothing else.

To the grandmother he allowed two shillings and sixpence per month, but made no provision for fuel, lodgings, nutritious diet, or cordials — all of which this old woman much required.

When I visited the house where old Flora Matheson and her grandchildren reside, I found her lying on a miserable pallet of straw, which with a few rags of clothing, are on the bare floor.

She is reduced to a skeleton, and I have no hesitation in declaring that she was then actually starving.

She had nothing whatever in the way of food but a few wet potatoes and two or three shellfish.

The picture she presented, as she lay on her wretched pallet of black rags and brown straw, with her mutch as black as soot, and her long arms thrown across, with nothing on them but the skin, was a most lamentable one — and one that reflects the deepest discredit on the parochial authorities of Strath.

There was no-one to attend to the wants or infirmities of this aged pauper but her grandchild, a young girl, ten years of age".

THE CROFTERS

MARY EVANS PICTURE LIBRARY, LONDON

CHAPTER 4

R.R. McIan's Victorian illustration from 'Clans of the Scottish Highlands'. Although bound for Canada, the rueful appearance of this emigrant could apply to any destination. Some emigrants, sailing in squalid conditions, failed to reach their new homeland alive and those that did often encountered formidable difficulties.

The Life of the Crofters

By Ernest McIntyre

The romantic notion that the introduction of crofting to the Highlands and Islands of Scotland brought an idyllic existence to people who could live happily off the harvests of land and sea and spend evenings in song and story, is unfortunately far from reality.

The stark truth is that the vast majority were forced to undertake backbreaking toil in a constant fight for survival against hunger, famine and the rigours of a harsh climate, poorly clad and badly housed, and all the while exploited by greedy landowners or leaseholders.

Yet, in spite of everything, they were able to preserve a dignity and bearing, a pride in lineage and a sense of hospitality which was admired by visitors to the crofting areas.

Paradoxically, crofting was a consequence of the notorious Clearances of the latter part of 18th and early 19th Centuries when half a million people were forcibly uprooted from lands they had cultivated for centuries to make way for sheep.

With the eradication of the clan system following the crushing of the Jacobite Rebellion of 1745, chiefs still owning land and new owners who had taken over from the dispossessed, saw big money was to be made in producing wool for the growing manufacturing towns of the south.

For years the clan lands had been worked communally, with groups sharing the available arable land for crop growing and upland grazings for their black cattle. Though the life was spartan, people were generally happy and in good health.

However, when the Clearances began, landowners realised that at least some labour would have to be retained to exploit what was then becoming another valuable profit source for the Highlands and Islands — the harvesting of seaweed for the making of kelp, an alkali essential for the production of soap.

As kelping was a seasonal occupation, landowners introduced the crofting system whereby individual families were allotted small portions of land but only enough to provide them with the barest of existence.

This was done deliberately so that crofters would have to pledge their labour for kelping and other tasks to pay their rents or to buy implements or extra food needed to stave off starvation.

Crofts were grouped together in small "townships" with a community-elected constable to maintain a semblance of law and order and to settle disputes.

Houses were built of turf and sometimes of stone if available. Roofs were thatched with heather, rushes of straw with a small hole left to allow smoke to escape from the peat fire constantly burning in the center of the main living area.

Gables were rounded to withstand storms sweeping in from the Atlantic and for the same reason walls, sometimes up to six feet thick, were kept small. Windows, where such existed, were tiny and heavily shuttered to keep out the frequent cold blasts, and for the same reason doors were kept low although often ill-fitting.

A Crofting Village.

In winter, the cow or other grazing animals would be housed in one end of a building, humans and beasts entering by the same door. Hens would roost in the warmth of the rafters and perhaps a goose or two would nest in recesses in the inner walls which were lime-washed to give some semblance of cleanliness.

Families, the old and the young, would huddle round the first at night in the glow from the peat fire and the crusie — and open iron lamp filled with fish oil and with a rush for a wick.

Constantly enveloped in peat smoke, they would share their meagre supplies of food, eating from wooden bowls with horn spoons, before exchanging the many tales of times that were always better in the days of long ago.

Cooking pots hung from a chain or bar over the fire, an iron rack was used for grilling fish, flat girdles (gridles) for scones and oatcakes and baking was possible in primitive peat ovens.

Oatmeal, milk, eggs — and later potatoes when they were introduced from Ireland — were the ingredients from which an amazing variety of dishes could be concocted. Fresh fish was to be had if the croft was near the sea and sea birds were also eaten.

Kale, seaweed, nettles and other plants could be used for soups but meat was rarely available unless a sheep kept for its wool for spinning died or when game was poached when the game-keeper's back was turned.

Box beds were the usual sleeping places. These had storage places at the bottom with adults sleeping in the middle and children on top. Despite the close mixing of different ages and sexes, great care was taken to preserve a strict decorum.

Other furniture in the home might consist of a sideboard with shelves and plate-rack for wooden food vessels and crockery if this could be obtained.

Crofters were adept at making ropes from heather and other materials and at weaving baskets of all sizes for indoor and outdoor uses. The same skill was seen in the wickerwork sides of household good containers which maintained a flow of air.

Clothing was rough homespun, women wearing dark skirts with a blouse and generally a shawl or a plaid, a long piece of wollen cloth worn over the shoulder. A spotless white cap was kept to adorn heads on special occasions.

Men wore trousers of heavy, dark cloth — the kilt was banned after the 1745 Rebellion and when the Act was repealed many Highlanders never went back to wearing it. Both sexes wore cloth stockings.

Hidden among the rocks on the remote hillsides would be the illicit whisky stills where liquor was made for home consumption as well as for export.

Outsmarting the Government's excise officers made an exciting diversion in an otherwise drab existence. Bribes offered in efforts to trap offenders were rarely accepted for fear of communal ostracism. Ale could also be brewed from barley of heather.

Skilled work which the crofters could not carry out themselves was done by itinerant craftsmen — blacksmiths, carpenters, wheelwrights, stonemasons, boatbuilders and others — who travelled from settlement to settlement and received hospitality during their stay.

Tuberculosis, diptheria and smallpox claimed many victims young and old among crofters as they did in other parts of Scotland, but for the treatment of lesser ills Highlanders had a proven faith in the curative properties of many plants.

People in the townships were very dependent on each other, and the old, the sick and the young were cared for to an extent that often called for tremendous personal sacrifice.

Despite the hardships and constant struggle against the elements, the people had no desire to escape from their environment and no joy was shown by the many thousands forced to emigrate overseas or to join highland Regiments, the Royal Navy, the Merchant Navy or to take work in the factories of the south.

With so many men away, women were often the mainstay of the family and taking more than their due of the heaviest toil.

Much of the work was therefore done communally, like turning the soil, harvesting, cutting the peat, and herding the animals at summer grazings which, like kelping, took many people away from home.

Kelping was perhaps the most grievous task that men, women and even young children had to endure.

One observer described it thus: "If one figures to himself a man, and one or or more of his children, engaged from morning to night in cutting, drying and otherwise preparing the sea weeds, at a distance of many miles from his home, or in a remote island; often for hours together wet to the knees and elbows; living upon oatmeal and water and occasionally fish, limpets and crabs; sleeping on the damp floor of a wretched hut; and with no other fuel than twigs or heath; he will perceive that this manufacture is none of the most agreeable."

Although crofters were indispensable for the harvesting and processing of the seaweed, landlords, who had the sole means of disposal, paid them the most meagre wages and much of these had to be paid back as rent for the crofts.

Peat cutting, though hard, was a happier communal activity. In doing so the crofters were not only ensuring their winter warmth but the operation took crofters away from the dreariness of normal daily chores.

After men cut the peat, women and children laid it out to dry and there would be a mid-day break for a picnic of bannocks and cheese with buttermilk for the young and tea brewed from heather roots for the adults.

Later the peat was stacked near the homesteads to make it accessible in winter months.

Waulking was another enjoyable get together for women. It was a process to shrink the woven cloth and involved a group thumping and turning it in time to their songs, many of which are still used today.

Indeed crofters had special songs to lighten many of their day-to-day tasks. It was said that without the soothing croon of a milkmaid cows would not give of their best.

A number of annual events were eagerly anticipated. At Beltane, the time for pasturing the cows and sowing the Spring seed, special food would be prepared and young girls would wash faces in the dawn dew in the hope of acquiring lasting beauty.

Samhain marked the gathering of the harvest and the return of herds from the hills. Flames were brought from the hillside fires to rekindle those in the households.

Hogmanay, New Year's Eve, was a time of general good cheer and was marked by many strange rituals which varied widely in different areas. Christmas was more of a religious festival and was observed according to the old calendar on what is now known as Twelfth Night.

Ceilidhs were frequent happy gatherings in winter. Neighbours bearing small offerings of food or fuel would gather in a chosen house to entertain themselves with songs, poems and stories, true and imagined, women carrying on with their knitting the while.

If there was no fiddler, a form of mouth-music would provide the rhythm for dancing, and refreshments would be passed round during the evening. Bagpipes were for the private pipers of the chiefs and more wealthy landowners.

Then, of course, there were the Highland weddings which were accompanied by celebrations lasting for days with the whole community contributing food and drink.

On the great day a white flag was flown from the roof of the bride's house and everyone gathered at the church or

CROFTERS HOME

minister's manse before repairing to a decorated bar or other suitable place where nights and days were danced away until food, drink and humans were completely exhausted.

In summer, daytime pastimes for men included a form of shinty and trials of strength of various kinds which developed into the traditional sports now seen at today's Highland Games.

In the latter part of the 19th Century the many grievances and hardships crofters had to endure began to be made known to a wider world largely through the efforts of a newspaper named The Highlander which was founded by John Murdoch of Inverness in 1873.

Despite fears of eviction, crofters themselves began to protest and there were some violent confrontations between tenants and agents or supporters of proprietors. At times police and troops had to be brought in to quell uprisings.

Then came a Royal Commission to examine the conditions and in 1886 the Crofters Holdings (Scotland) Act established long overdue rights including security of tenure, fair rents, compensations for improvements and the ability to hand down a croft to another member of the family.

Subsequent legislation has done much to improve the life of crofters who today enjoy a free and independent way of life while forming a important part of the Highland economy.

REPAIRING THE ROOF — 1890.

THE TARTAN

THE TARTAN

Here's to it:
    The fighting sheen of it,
The yellow, the green of it,
    The white, the blue of it,
The swing, the hue of it,
Every thread of it:

The fair have sighed for it,
    The brave have died for it,
Foemen sought for it,
    Heroes fought for it,
Honour the name of it,
    Drink to the fame of it--
The Tartan

           -Murdoch Maclean

CHAPTER 5

ROSS TARTAN

The evolution of Highland dress, with acknowledgements to the Museum of Scottish Tartans, Comrie

C 1570 — After 1600 — Late 17 Century — After 1600 — Early 18 Century

✚✚✚✚✚ ROSS ✚✚✚✚✚

Cromarty Manuscript p.11

Rosse he hath ae minglit sette and ain redd sett and the mingt hathe fyrst on ylk syd twa wyd stryppes of blew quhairunto cvmenthe twa sprainges of grene and yrefter twa stryppis o greine the quhilk be the mydwarde of the hail sette for the scarlat sett ther goethe yron sax spraingis of blew thre and the thegiddir and the midward of ilk thre ys ever the grossest.

Setts: 220   **Vestiarium Scotticum p.78P17**

Clan Anrias. He hath ae minglit sett and ae redd sett. and the minglit sett hathe fyrst on ylk syd yroff twa stryppis of blew, quhairvnto cvmethe twa sprangis of grene, and yrefter twa stryppis of grein, ye quhilk be medwarde of ye haill sett, for ye scarlatt sett thair gangeth yron thre spraingis blew, and ye mydward of ye thre ys euer ye grossest.

Count, after PL.7   G R G R B R B R G R G R
                                    4 6 2 566 2 6 8 2 4 24 6

FROM: Scotland's Forged Tartans by Donald C. Stuart & J.C. Thompson, publ. by Paul Harris, E'burgh 1980

(Yestiarium - cont. pg.4)

THE ROSS TARTANS

Ancient Hunting *Ross*

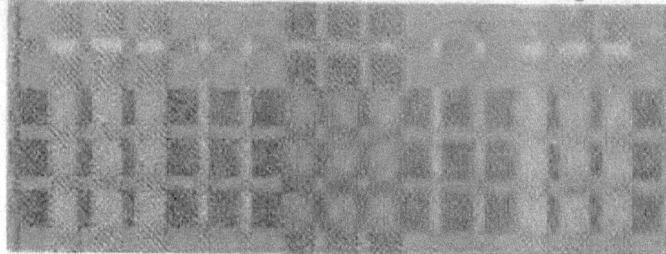
Ancient Ross

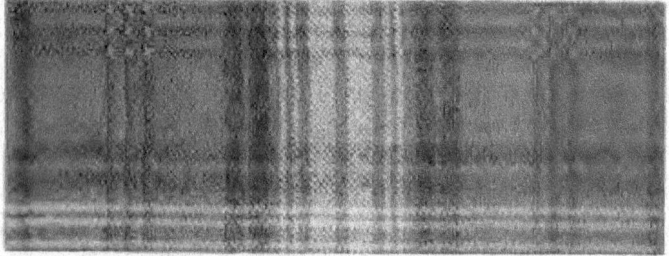
Modern Hunting

Modern Ross

ROSS

There have been references in Highland literature to tartans for several hundred of years and it is therefore safe to assume that they were known to the people for at least a similar period. The word "tartan" can be taken to mean "striped", "mottled" or "chequered", the Gaelic word for it is breacan which means "chequered" and describes the check-like patterns. When the word "sett" is used in reference to a tartan we mean the pattern; a length of tartan is composed of one "sett" repeated over and over again until one has the desired length. The early tartans were part of the dress of Scottish people but it was in the Highlands that they became associated with clans. At first they were simple checks of two or three colors which were obtained from dye-producing plants. When chemical dyes came into use the colors became more elaborate. Originally, the simple checks were worn by the people of a district and these became known as "district tartans", the oldest of the tartans. Since the people in a district usually belonged to a clan the district tartan often became a clan tartan. Some care was taken to keep a record of the tartan setts and in time the people of each district could be identified by the pattern of their tartan.

One of the earliest references to tartan is during the reign of James 111 in 1471 when a number of yards were purchased for the King and Queen. Perhaps the first clan tartan to be so recognized was the MacLean hunting tartan for there is reference to "sixty ells of cloth of white, black and green colours" in a matter of good taste come to the fore. Scots should be complimented when they see others who, for one reason or another, wish to wear a certain tartan. There are few who may object to this but the majority of Scots have enough common sense to know that you cannot legislate in such matters.

The basic garment until about 1500 was a shirt probably of linen, the length of which could be regulated by a belt. If one so desired, tight fitting trousers could be worn underneath this mantle which, among Scottish Gaels by 1400, was striped, or a tartan. Shortly after the 1600 the Scots were belting this mantle so that the lower part formed a kilt above the knees and the upper part was hitched to the shoulder. This top part could be used for protection in cold weather. This was the plaid and was known as the belted plaid; by the early 1700s the kilted part was hand pleated by the wearer. Around the same time the lower part became belted on as a kilt and worn seperately from the top half. Then the pleats were stitched in and the army began to iron the pleats. The modern kilt therefore. though much more refined and considerably more expensive, is derived from the belted plaid. The women also wore a belted plaid which reached the ankles with the top part draped so as to fall softly from the shoulders. The kilt as we know it is of fairly recent orgin but the tartans can be easily traced back for as least 500 years. The short modern kilt refers to something "girded" or "tucked up" and is actually a Danish word. It is a translation of the Gaelic word "fileadh" and was originally applied to the "fileadh mor" meaning "great Fileadh" or "belted plaid". Today the term often used is "feileadh beag" or "philabeg", meaning "little kilt". It is generally believed that this little kilt was perhaps first used around 1700; it was fairly common by 1746 but authorities still disagree as to the exact date of its introduction. It was probable that they found it more practical in working or in fighting than the larger belted plaid. Sometime Highlanders were refered to as "REDSHANKS" because of their custom of going barefooted and barelegged and their ability to endure cold weather. Occasionally some wore boots which went as high as their knees and others wore a form of sandal made of animal hide.

THE DYES OF EARLY TARTANS

Original tartan colours were not the clear, intense ones so often associated with them now. Rather, the old time tartans were coloured "bright but soft", according to James D. Scarlett in *How to Weave Fine Cloth*. He goes on to describe, "a rather light scarlet; a deeper red, the color of the wild rose; a strong, very slightly 'muddy' yellow; a dark (but by no means black) blue; and a green that might be sage, reséda or olive of medium depth. Light blue was represented by shades varying from light blue-grey to duck-egg blue (which was the most usual). A much used color that was completely lost in the transition was a warm dark blue called purple in its day, although it was very unlike our modern color of the same name. Even bleached wool is inclined to revert to a slightly creamy color with age.

In an unpublished master's thesis, Mary Etta MacDonald speaks of the dyestuffs of the early Scottish, weavers. Research has shown, she says, that the Highland dyer was able to produce most colors satisfactorily from the plants available in her own glen. The truest and fastest blue was from the leaves of Devil's bit (*Scabiosa succisa*). Other blue tone dyes were from the root of the yellow iris (*Iris pseudacorus*) and the berry of the elderberry tree mordanted with alum. The most common native red was from the roots of ladies' bedstraw (*Galuim verum*) mordanted with alum, but it was not as brilliant as madder red. The lichen *Lencanora tartarea* yielded red when steeped with urine for three weeks.

Lichens were much used by Highlanders and were substantive dyes (not requiring a mordant). A late 16th century writer described the use of "scurf" or lichen in the Western Isles:

"This scurf dyes a pretty crimson color; first well dried, and then ground to powder, after which it is steeped in urine,. . . and in three weeks it is ready to boil with the yarn that is to be dyed."

The best purple was from cudbear, a preparation of two lichens fermented with fual and potash. Lichens were also a source for yellows, though some of the best yellows were from the flowers of heather (*Erica vulgaris*) and broom (*Sarothamnus scoparius*). A dark yellow came from the bracken root (*Pteris aquilina*). All shades of green were produced overdyeing; privet berries *(Ligustrum vulgare)* were also said to give a bright green with alum mordant.

Browns were obtained from tree bark, such as the tannin-rich oak, but the richest and fastest browns came from lichens. One species is still used to dye some Harris tweeds in the Outer Hebrides.

The most difficult colours to obtain from native dyestuffs were blue and red. These two colors were imported at an early date; indigo blue was imported before 1700, and woad, an even earlier foreign blue vegetable dye, was probably obtained from Holland. Madder was imported from Flanders and used extensively. . .

Excerpted from The Scottish Tartan in Modern Dress *by Mary Etta MacDonald, an unpublished master's thesis. Colorado State University, Fort Collins, CO. August, 1967.*

Scabiosa succisa

HIGHLAND DRESS IN THE 1700'S
Men's Dress

The Highland Dress consists of a bonnet made of thrum without a brim, a short coat, a waistcoat, longer by five of six inches, short stockings, and Brogues, or pumps without heels. By the way, they cut holes in their brogues, though new made, to let out the water; when they have far to go and rivers to pass; this they do to preserve their feet from galling. Few besides gentlemen wear the Trowze, that is, the breeches and stockings all of one piece, and drawn on together; over this habit they wear a plaid, which is usually three yards long and two breadths wide, and the whole garb is made of chequered tartan, or plaiding; this, with the Sword and pistol, is called a full dress, and, to a well-proportioned man, with any tolerable air, it makes an agreeable figure; but this you have seen in London, and it is chiefly their mode of dressing when they are in the Lowlands, or when they make a neighbouring visit, or go anywhere on horseback; but when those among them who travel on foot, and have not attendants to carry them over the waters, they vary it into the Quelt, which is a manner I am about to describe.

The common habit of the ordinary highlanders is far from being acceptable to the eye; with them a small part of the plaid, which is not so large as the former, is set into folds and girt around the waist, to make of it a short petticoat that reaches half way down the Thigh, and the rest is brought over the shoulders, and then fastened before, below the neck, often with a fork and sometimes with a bodkin or sharpened piece of stick, so that they make pretty nearly the Appearance of the poor women in London when they bring their gowns over their heads to shelter them from the rain. In this way of wearing the plaid, they have sometimes nothing else to cover them, and are often barefoot; but some I have soon shod with a kind of pumps, made out of a raw cow-hide, with the hair turned outward, which being ill-made, the wearer's foot looked something like those of a rough-footed hen or pigeon; these are called Quarrants, and are not only offensive to the sight but intolerable to the smell of those who are near them. The stocking rises no higher than the Thick of the Calf, and from the Middle of the thigh to the middle of the leg is a naked space, which being exposed to all weathers, becomes tanned and freckled and the joint being mostly infected with the country distemper, the whole is very disagreeable to the eye. This dress is called the Quelt; (editor — kilt in today's language) and, for the most part they wear the petticoat so very short, that in a windy day going up a hill or stooping, the indecency of it is plainly discovered.

A highland gentleman told me one day merrily, as we were speaking of a dangerous precipice we had passed over together, that a lady of a noble family had complained to him very seriously, that as she was going over the same place with a Gilly, who was upon an upper path leading her horse with a long string, she was so terrified with the sight of the abyss, that, to avoid it, she was forced to look up toward the bare highlander all the way long.

I have observed before, that the plaid serves the ordinary people for a Cloak by day and bedding at night: By the latter it imbibes so much perspiration, that no one day can free it from the filthy smell; and even some of better than ordinary appearance, when the plaid falls from the shoulder, or otherwise requires to be readjusted, while you are talking with them, toss it over again, as some people do the knots of their wigs, which conveys the offence in whiffs that are intolerable; of this they seem not to be sensible, for it is often done only to give themselves airs.

Various reasons are given both for and against the Highland Dress. It is urged against it, that it distinguishes the natives as a body of people distinct and separate from the rest of the subjects of Great Britian, and thereby is one cause of their narrow adherence among themselves, to the exclusion of all the rest of the kingdom; but the part of the habit chiefly objected to is the plaid (or mantle), which they say, is calculated for the encouragement of an idle life in lying about upon the heath, in the day-time, instead of following some lawful employment; that it serves to cover them in the night when they lie in wait among the mountains, to commit their robberies and depredations; and is composed of such colours as altogether, in the mass, so nearly resemble the heath on which they lie, that it is hardly to be distinguished from it until one is so near them as to be within their power, if they have any evil intention; that it renders them ready at a moment's warning, to join in any rebellion as they carry continually their tents about them; and lastly, it was thought necessary, in Ireland, to supress that habit by Act of Parliament, for the above reasons, and no complaint for the want of it now remains among the Mountaineers of the Country.

On the other hand, it is alleged, the dress is most convenient to those who, with no ill design are obliged to travel from one part to another upon their lawful occasions, viz — That they would not be so free to skip over the rocks and bogs with breeches as they are in the short petticoat; that it would be greatly incommodious to those who are frequently to wade through waters, to wear breeches, which must be taken off upon every such occurrence, or would not only gall the wearer, but render it very unhealthful and dangerous to their limbs, to be constantly wet in that part of the body; especially in Winter-time, when they might be frozen and with respect to the plaid in particular, the distance between one place of shelter and another, is often too great to be reached before night comes and, being intercepted by sudden floods, or hindered by other impediments, they are frequently obliged to lie all night in the hills, in which case they must perish, were it not for the covering they carry with them. That even if they should be so fortunate as to reach some hospitable hut, they must lie upon the ground uncovered, there being nothing to do spared from the family for that purpose.

And to conclude, a few shillings will buy this dress for an ordinary highlander, who very probably, might hardly ever be in condition to purchase a lowland suit, though of the coarsest cloth or stuff, fit to keep him warm in that cold climate.

Burt's letters from the North of Scotland
c1730

MEN'S FORMAL DRESS—MALE HIGHLAND DRESS

Montrose doublet   Sherriffmuir coat   Prince Charlie Coatee   Regulation Doublet   Kenmore Doublet

1. Montrose Doublet:
   Velvet or cloth, black or of a colour to blend with the kilt. Silver buttons or Celtic design, leather belt with silver buckle, lace jabot.

2. Sheriffmuir Coat:
   Velvet or cloth, black or of a colour to blend with the kilt. Silver buttons, matching or tartan vest, white shirt with turn-down collar or stiff shirt with wing collar, black bow tie or lace jabot.

3. Prince Charlie Coatee:
   Black cloth with silk facings or velvet of a colour to blend with the kilt; silver buttons, matching or tartan vest; white shirt with turn-down collar or stiff shirt with wing collar; black bow tie or lace jabot.
   Lace ruffles at the cuffs may be worn when the jabot is worn. A silver brooch mounted with cairngorms may be worn on the jabot.
   Shean Dhu is worn in the stocking on the right leg.
   Green or red garters and flashes must be worn.
   For dancing, black ghillie shoes should be worn otherwise the shoes should be patent leather dress brogues with strap and buckle or 'gillie' lacing.

4. Regulation Doublet:
   Black cloth, peak or notch lapels, silk facings, silver buttons, matching or tartan vest, shoulder straps, gauntlet cuffs and Inverness flaps, Shirt as for Prince Charlie Coatee.

5. Kenmore Doublet:
   Cloth or velvet, black or of a colour to blend with the kilt. Single breasted with a stand collar and lace jabot.

With thanks to "Scotland Through Her Country Dances"
George S. Emmerson

LADIES FORMAL DRESS—THE SASH

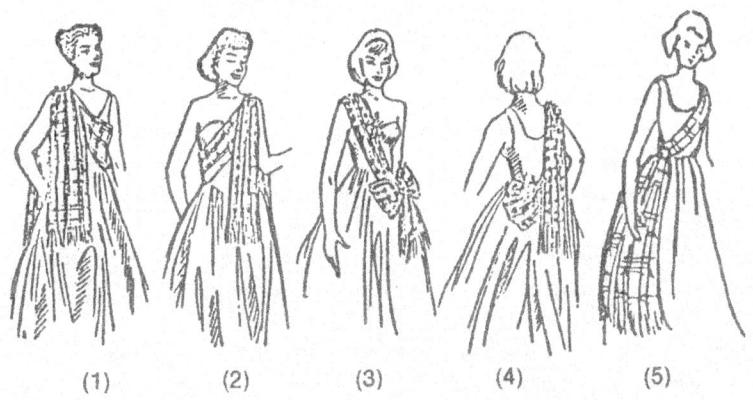

(1)   (2)   (3)   (4)   (5)

1. Style worn by Clanswomen:
   The sash is worn over the right shoulder across the breast of the waist, across the back over the right shoulder and is secured by a pin or small brooch on the right shoulder.
2. Style worn by wives of Clans Chiefs and wives of Colonels of the Scottish Regiments:
   The sash, which may be reather fuller (24 inches wide with 12 inch fringe) is worn over the left shoulder across the breast to the waist across the back over the left shoulder and secured with a brooch on the left shoulder.
3. Style worn by ladies who have married out of their Clan:
   Ladies who wish to use their original clan tartan. The sash, usually longer than style 1, is worn over the right shoulder, secured there with a pin and fastened in a large bow on the left hip.
4. For Country Dancing or where the lady wishes to keep the front of her dress free:
   The sash is attached to the dress at the back of the waist, perhaps by a small belt, and at the right shoulder by a pin or brooch so that the ends fall backward from the right shoulder and hand behind the right arm.
5. For Country Dancing or where the lady wishes to have free movement of her limbs.
   The sash is worn over the left shoulder and gathered at the right waist with a pin or brooch, or under a belt.
   FOR SCOTTISH COUNTRY DANCING: the usual costume is a white dress, with the sash - not very wide - over the right shoulder, and tied with a loose knot under the left arm, fringed ends, one longer than the other. A sash, not long should be placed round the waist and tied behind.

PUTTING ON THE KILT

Nowdays "putting on the kilt" is no great problem. You simply slip the fabric round your waist and do up the buckles. Unless, of course, you've added a little weight to yourself since the last time you wore the garment. In such a case it helps to have a good wife who'll poke and prod and finally get the buckles done up — or who'll lend you one of her "undergarments"— to "suck up the fat".

At one time "the plaid" was simply a very large piece of cloth which one had to artfully and carefully wrap round himself.

The following diagrams will give those adventurous among you the opportunity to wear a GREAT KILT. How long it will stay on you, is a matter of how diligently you follow the steps involved in putting it on. For a good GREAT KILT you need at least six yards of plaid (tartan).

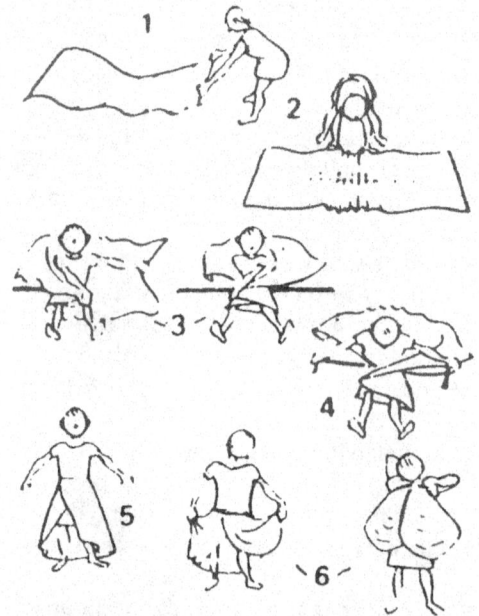

1. Place your plaid on the floor with one of your largest belts beneath it.

2. Plait or gather the cloth towards the middle of the piece.

3. Lay down on the gathered portion of the cloth, making sure that your belt (beneath the cloth) is at your waistline. Spread both your arms

100

and grasp the edges of the cloth in your hands. Fold first the right side over yourself and then the left.

4. Spread your arms and find your belt. Bring your belt around your middle and do it up as tightly as you can at your waistline (otherwise you'll be in trouble! if the belt is above or below your waist line, you'll lose your Great Kilt as soon as you stand up which is the next step.

5. Stand up carefully. You'll now be wearing a skirt of sorts. Bend down and with a hand on each side pick up the bottom corner of the material on the left and right sides of you that is touching the floor. Bring this material up to your left shoulder.

6. With a large, decorative pin, secure this material to your left shoulder. You have enough material that if it rains all you need to do is undo the pin and pull all the material over your shoulders and down your front to make a cape-like covering.

7. Now don't you feel like the Highlander!

THE CLAYMORE

ROSS

CHAPTER 6

Broadswords, Dirks and Sgian-Dubhs

Interesting swords and knives were brought to America by these people and by the military forces of the Revolutionary War. The Claymore, a huge Scottish greatsword of the 16th century, gave its name to the smaller broadsword of the 17th and 18th centuries.

Universally identified with the Scots, the broadsword had a distinctive basket type hilt, said to have originated in eastern Europe. Early hilts were made of heavy iron strips which gave excellent protection to the hand. Later the bars were rounder and more ornate.

The straight double-edged blade was about 33 inches long, 1¼ inches wide and usually had a fuller. Names or mottos were often inscribed on the blade. "Andria Farara" was frequently seen. This was probably the work of a German blade maker with an eye to the Scottish trade. "Prosperity to Scotland and No Union" was a motto which referred to a union of the Scottish and English parliaments in 1707.

This weapon served well through two centuries. With the advent of more reliable and accessible firearms, it became less useful and in 1834, the Claymore was reserved for full dress only.

A companion piece to the broadsword was the Scottish dirk. Patterned after the Saxon scramasax and the ballock knife, it evolved into the middle of the 17th century. Like it's predecessors, it had no guard and was single edged. The overall length was usually about 18 inches but some were as short as 12 inches.

Earlier blades were often made of cut down broadswords, thus had a fuller. This feature is present in those of later periods. The top of the back edge, was notched or scalloped from the hilt to midway down the blade.

While ivory or horn were used for hilts on older dirks, most were wood, carved with a Celtic design. The sheath was leather covered wood. Both the hilt and the scabbard were trimmed with metal mounts, finished in Scottish motifs, and sometimes with family or regimental crests. The top of the pommel was decorated with a faceted cairngorm of a metal cap. Often the sheath was made to accommodate a knife and fork. These, of course, were for dining while the dirk was used for self defense or more mundane purposes.

As with the broadsword, when the dirk outlived its useful purpose, it was relegated to a symbolic piece. Today, it is an interesting adjunct to form Scottish attire.

The sgian-dudbh, Gaelic for black knife, and pronounced "Sken due", is still another intriguing Scottish institution. Having no guard or belt fastenings, it was first carried in the sleeve and later in the top of the stocking. Here it was easily accessible and added a decorative touch to the Highland raiment. Its main function was that of a weapon or skinning knife.

The black wooden hilt was carved on the face with a woven pattern, while the back was smooth, presumably to allow the knife to be easily drawn in an emergency. A cairngorm often decorated the top of the pommel.

The sheath was wood with a black leather covering. Both the hilt and the sheath had metal mounts which were either plain of tastefully designed.

The 3 inch or 4 inch blade was single edged and the back side was notched and often bore a false edge as did the dirk, Following tradition, the blade had a fuller. The sgian-dudh is still worn with Highland apparel.

Since the inception of the Claymore, dirk, and sgian-dudh, there have been countless changes. In speaking with knowledgeable Scots and in researching available information, many contradictions were encountered. To the Scottish purist who finds any discrepencies, please understand.

Printed by permission of Knife World P.O. Box 3395, Knoxville, Tennessee 37917.

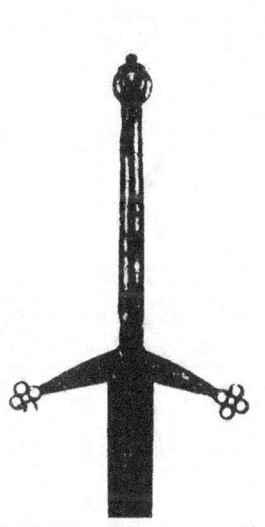

Early 16th century claymore with wheel pommel.

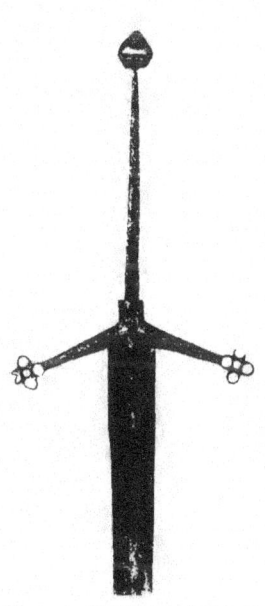

Claymore with globular pommel, second half of 16th century.

HIGHLAND DANCING, MUSIC AND POEMS

CHAPTER 7

Highland Dancing

When interest in competition Highland Dancing grew with the passing years, instruction became authoritative and the dancing technique became more defined. Since there were differing ideas on technique and judging, the Scottish Official Board of Highland Dancing and its traditional and accepted technique of competition came into being.

Competitive dancers today are judged on the prescribed technique of the SOBHD. The dancers are awarded "points" for appearance, poise, the position of the hands and feet, and the execution of the intricate steps. For example, when a dancer raises his leg, bent at the knee, instead of lifting the knee forward or the foot backward he should raise the knee sideways and keep it well pressed back. In this position the apron of the kilt still remains flat and more or less in the original position.

The Highland Fling

The Highland Fling originated as a wild dance of triumph following victory in battle. It is said to be inspired by the capers of a stag, the dancer's upraised arms representing the animal's antlers. Danced vigorously and exultantly, it is now highly stylized and calls for the greatest skill in technique and exactness of timing. Despite the variety of steps, it should, for example, be danced throughout in the same position on the board, perhaps because originally the Highland Fling was said to have been done on the shield of the clansman. It has become the classic solo dance at modern competitive dancing events, and is often selected at competitions to decide who will be judged the best Highland dancer of the day.

The Sword Dance

Like the Highland Fling, the Sword Dance, or Ghillie Chalium, has war as its basic theme. Today it is both picturesque and popular at Highland Games; legend has it that in older times it was danced on the eve of battle, and that for the soldier to touch or displace his sword portended evil in the coming fight. There are many other theories regarding the origin of the Sword Dance, and one of the most attractive of these is that which tells how the great Malcolm Canmore, after having defeated one of Macbeth's chiefs at the battle of Dunsinane in 1054, seized his opponent's sword, placing it over his own to form a cross, over which he danced triumphantly to the wild music of the pipes.

Seann Triubhas

The Seann Triubhas is associated with the period from 1746 to 1782 when, following the rebellion of 1745, the Scots were forbidden to wear their ancient Highland Dress, and had instead to wear the despised trousers. Seann Triubhas (prounounced Shawn Truews) merely means "without trousers." The first part of the dance, which is one of gracefull, flowing movements, is supposed to mock the restrictions imposed by the foreign trousers, while the second part exhibits the freedom of action possible when wearing the kilt.

Reels

Unlike the three previous dances which are all solo dances, the dances classified as reels have always been group dances for recreational rather than military purposes. There are many variations, but the reel is always one of the most stirring events at modern Highland Games. Legend has it that the reel originated outside a locked church, where it was danced by chilly parishioners as a method of keeping warm while waiting for a tardy clergyman.

Pipe Music

The only Pipe Tunes associated with the Clan Ross are *The Earl of Ross's March* and *Salute to the Earl of Ross,* said by the late Reverend Neil Ross, D.D., of Laggan, Inverness-shire (a native of Skye, and a fine player on the pipes) to have been composed by Donald Mor MacCrimmon, hereditary piper to Sir Roderick Mor MacLeod of Dunvegan. It may be stated here that the Clan Ross has produced several excellent pipers. One was William Ross, a native of Ross-shire, who was a piper to Queen Victoria from 1854 till his death in 1891. In 1876 he published a collection of pipe music, containing forty-one piobaireachds and 437 marches, strathspeys and reels. A second edition appeared in 1885.

THE BAGPIPE

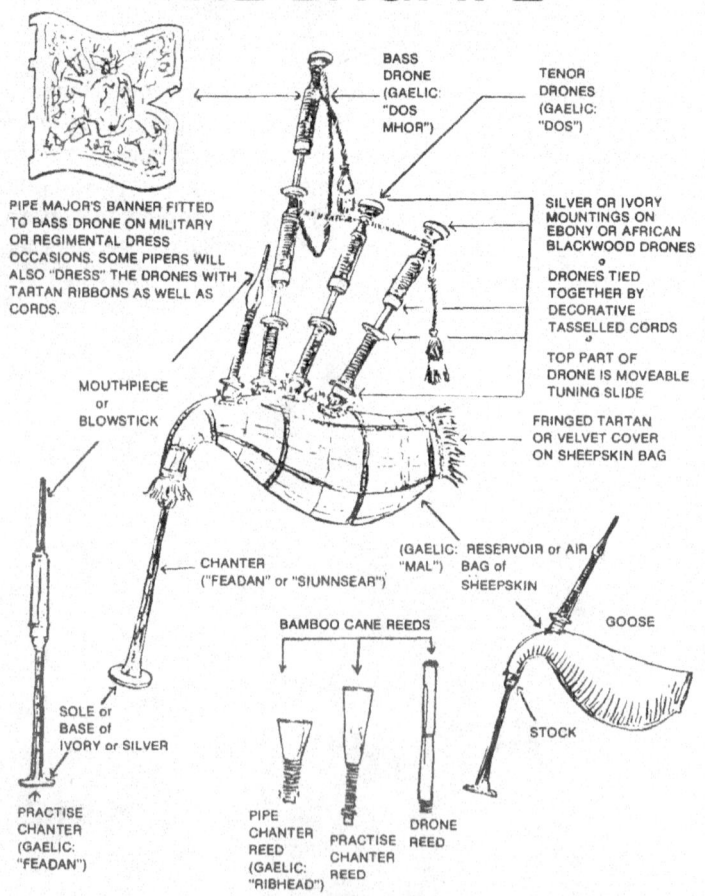

For our many **"Great Ross Pipers"**---

"Playing the bagpipe within doors," says General Stewart, is a Lowland and English custom. In the Highlands the piper is always in the open air; and when people wish to dance to his music, it is on the green, if the weather permits; nothing but necessity makes them attempt a pipe-dance in the house. The bagpipes was a field instrument intended to call the clans to arms, and animate them in battle, and was no more intended for a house than a round of six pounders. A broadside from a first-rate, or a round from a battery, has a sublime and impressive effect at a proper distance. In the same manner, the sound of bagpipes, softened by distance, had an indescribable effect on the mind and action of the Highlanders. But a few would choose to be under the muzzle of guns of a battery, so I have seldom seen a Highlander, whose ears were not grated when close to pipes, however much his breast might be warmed, and his feelings roused, by the sounds to which he had been accustomed in his youth when proceeding from the proper distance."

Spaidsearached Iarla Rois
The Earl of Ross's March

D.M. MacCRIMMON

I. Urlar

II. Var. I

III. Var. II Singling

IV. Var. II Doubling

SPAIDSEARACHD IARLA ROIS
(The Earl of Ross's March)

In the Canntaireachd (II—34) it is called Chean na Daise. The ground is the same as in Angus MacKay and the text. Then follow two Variations as follows:—

S. *First Motion*
Line 1st   Hiotro hiotro hiotroao hiharin hiharin hiotro hiotro hiotro dareehao drea hiodin,
" 2nd   Hiotro hiotro hiotroao hiharin hiharin hintodrea hihorodo hao drea hihorodo hihorodo hiotro hiotro hiotro daree hao drea hiodin,
" 3rd   Hiotro hiotro hiotroao hiharin hiharin dâreeha chetro daree hao drea hiodin hiharin four times.

D.
Line 1st   Chetro chetro chetroao hiharin hiharin chetro chetro chetro dâree hao drea hiodin,
" 2nd   Chetro chetro chetroao hiharin hiharin hintodrea hihorodo hao drea hihorodo hihorodo chetro chetro chetro dârcchao drea hiodin,
" 3rd   Chetro chetro chetroao hiharin hiharin dâreeha chetro dâree hao drea hiodin hiharin hiharin.

S. *Second*
Line 1st   Hinda hinto hinto hinda hiharin hiharin hinto hinto hinda hinda hinto hinda hiodin,
" 2nd   Hinda hinto hinto hinda hiharin hiharin hinto hinda hihorodo hinda hinda hihorodo hihorodo hinda four times, Hinto hinda hiodin,
" 3rd   Hinda hinto hinto hinda hiharin hiharin hinto hinto hinda hinda hinto hinda hinda hinto hiharin four times.

D.
Line 1st   Hinda hinto hinda hinto hinda hinda hinto,
" 2nd   Hinda hinto hinda hinda hinto two times,
" 3rd   Hinda hinto, hinda hinto, hinda hinda hinto two times, hindariddan four times.

Then follow "Taolive Gear" and "Cruilive Fosgail," which differ slightly from Mackay's Variation 2 and Crunluath as follows:—
S.   *Taolive Gear*
Line 1st   Hindaenda hindaento hindaento hindaenda hiharin hiharin hindaento hindaento hindaenda hindaenda hindaento hindacnda hiodin,

" 2nd   Hindacnda hindaento hindaento hindaenda hiharin hiharin
        hindacnto hindaenda hihorodo hindaenda hindaenda hihorodo
        hihorodo hindaridda four times, hindaento hindaenda hiodin,
" 3rd   Hindaenda hindaento hindaento hindaenda hiharin hiharin hindaento
        hindaento hindaenda hindaenda hindaento hindaenda hindaenda
        hindaento, hiharin four times.
D.
Line 1st Hindacnda hindacnto hindacnda hindacnto hindaenda hindaenda
        hindacnto,
" 2nd   Hindacnda hindacnto,hindacnda hindaenda hindaento two times,
" 3rd   Hindacnda hindaento hindaenda hindaento hindaenda hindaenda,
        hindaento, two times, hindarid four times.

Crulive Fosgail
Take from Taolive Gear playing (1) hindadre for hindaenda, (2) hintodre for hindaento, (3) hindadre for hindaridda, (4) hinbandre for hindarid.

EDITORIAL NOTES

John,11th Earl of Ross and Lord of the Isles, is said by Angus MacKay to have surrendered the earldom to the Crown in 1476. Nevertheless, he dates the composition of this tune by Donald Mor MacCrimmon as about 1600. (The Clan MacCrimmon Society puts Donald Mor's birth year as c. 1570!)

This tune is in the Campbell Canntaireachd and also in Neil MacLeod of Gesto's small book of 1828, where it is entitled "Played at a time when the Scotts were at war in England and obliged to feed on the Ears of Corn for want of Provision commonly called Kieunidize," and where it is expressed in a slightly different form of Canntaireachd language.

Possibly there was some local celebrity, who called himself the Earl of Ross, but was not entitled to do so officially.

The first and second Variations as given in the Campbell Canntaireachd are appended.

The metre of the tune is a slight variant of that described in the Kilberry Book Introduction, p. 14, footnote. Here the third line is identical with line 1 in every part. The Crunluath Doubling has been copied exactly from Angus MacKay's book, but it is plain that bars 3 of each line should be played twice to match the rest of the tune.

Perhaps in the earlier days of the use of musical notation for pipe music, extra variations were evolved, either to satisfy the demand of youthful enthusiasts for appropriately noisy finales, or to prolong the execution of a piece on the field of battle. In particular, one of the symbols used (*e.g.*—the one called callach by General Thomason) may have been more readily fingered and timed by experts than described accurately by them on paper in doublings. This may have been the situation here, and may account for there being comparatively few examples in books like those of MacDonald and MacKay.

The time is also recorded in the MSS. of Donald MacDonald and Peter Reid. Reid notes that it won first prize at the Edinburgh competition in 1824 when played by Donald Serimgeour from Perthshire, and in 1826 by John Gordon, piper to the Atholl Club.

Ross of Pitcalnie   March

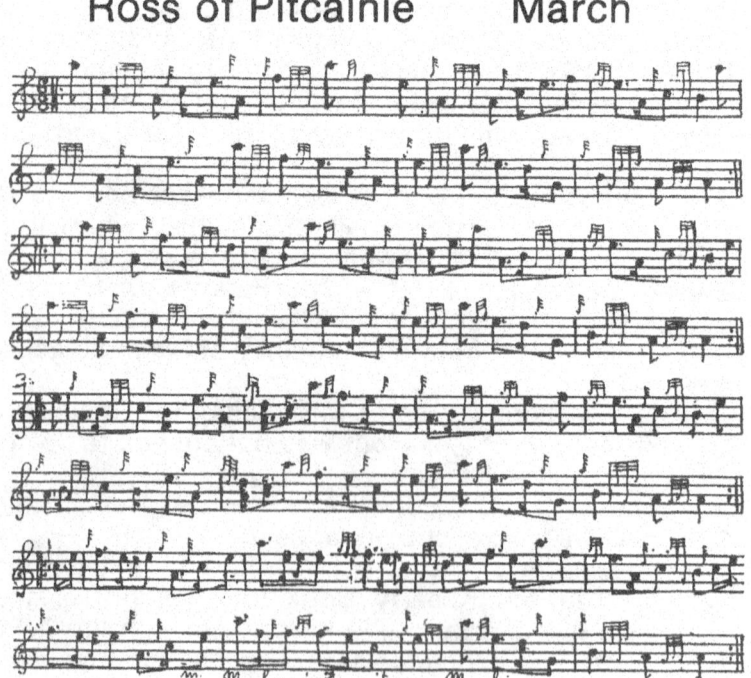

Simon Fraser's Manuscript

GESTO VII   "KIEUNIDIZE" – CEANN NA DEISE – HEADS OF CORN –
THE EARL OF ROSS'S MARCH

The Earl of Ross's March – Gesto VII

Simon Fraser called this tune 'Kiaunidize' or 'Kieunidize' which is a corruption for the Gaelic 'Ceann na deise', or in English — 'Heads of Corn'. He wrote that there are "two styles of this tune — the other ends with the first two bars of the urlar instead of four 'Hieririne' beats". It is this style presented here.

Mr. Harry Fraser has another setting of this tune written by his Uncle Simon and it showed these differences:-
(a) In the urlar — the note (a) is an 'E' not an 'F'
    - at (b), the cadence 'heodra' is played instead of 'hodra'.
    - at (c) 'hevihavi' instead of 'havihova'.

(b) The first variation is quite different and is written out in full.

(c) The second variation singling is as in the full tune but the doubling shows changes and is written out.

(d) This setting continues the theme from the doubling of variation two, through a variation three, and doubling, then Crunluigh Singling, and Doubling.

Gesto's Book is nearly identical with the full tune presented here but with these differences:—

-Bar 15 of Ground and 1st Variation has 'heiririn heiririn'
-In the first variation, bars 7 and 8 has 'heororo' repeated and apparently is played at double time?
-Bar 13 of first variation has 'bitri-o va, hindro bitri-o vao'.

Note the use of 'E' at the start of the tune and first variation. It is 'I' in the old notation and has religious significance. It is the tuning note before the actual music begins.

Songs of Scotland

Will Ye No Come Back Again

Bonnie Charlie's now awa',
    Safely owre the friendly main;
Mony a heart will break in twa,
    Should he ne'er come back again.

Will ye no come back again?
Will ye no come back again?
Better lo'ed ye canna be,
Will ye no come back again?

Ye trusted in your Hieland men,
    They trusted you, dear Charlie;
They kent you hiding in the glen,
    Your cleadin' was but barley.
        Will ye no &c.

English bribes were a' in vain,
    An e'en tho' puirer we may be;
Siller canna buy the heart
    That beats aye for thine and thee.
        Will ye no &c.

We watched thee in the gloamin' hour,
    We watched thee in the morning' grey;
Tho' thirty thousand pounds they'd gi'e,
    Oh there was nane that wad betray.
        Will ye no &c.

Sweet's the laverock's note and lang,;
    Lilting wildly up the glen;
But aye to me he sings ae sang,—
    Will ye no come back again?
        Will ye no &c.

Words by Lady Nairn

Bonnie Banks of Loch Lomond

By yon bonnie banks and by yon bonnie braes,
Where the sun shines bright on Loch Lomond
Where me and my true love were ever wont to gae,
On the bonnie, bonnie banks o'Loch Lomond.

Chorus
O ye'll tak' the high road and I'll tak' the low road,
And I'll be in Scotland afore ye.
But me and my true love will never meet again,
On the bonnie, bonnie banks o' Loch Lomond.

'Twas there that we parted in yon shady glen,
On the steep, steep side o' Ben Lomond.
Where in deep purple hue, the hieland hills we view,
And the moon comin' out in the gloamin'.

The wee birdies sing and the wild flowers spring,
And in sunshine the waters are sleeping:
But the broken heart it kens nae second spring again,
Tho' the waefu' may cease from their greeting.

Author not known.

Auld Lang Syne

Should auld acquaintance be forgot
   And never brought to mind?
Should auld acquaintance be forgot,
   And auld lang syne?

Chorus
For auld lang syne, my dear,
   For auld lang syne,
We'll tak' a cup o' kindness yet,
   For auld lang syne.

And surely ye'll be your pint-stoup,
   And surely I'll be mine;
And we'll tak' a cup o' kindness yet,
   For auld lang syne,
        For auld, &c.

We twa hae run about the braes,
   And pou'd the gowans fine;
But we've wandered mony a weary fit,
   Sin' auld lang syne.
        For auld, &c.

We twa hae paidl'd in the burn,
   Frae morning sun till dine;
But seas between us braid har roar'd,
   Sin' auld lang syne,
        For auld, &c.

And there's a hand, my trusty fiere!
   And gie's a hand o' thine!
And we'll tak' a right gude-willie waught,
   For auld lang syne,
        For auld, &c.

Words by Robert Burns

ADDRESS TO A HAGGIS

Fair fa' your honest sonsie face,
Great Chieftan o' the Puddin-race!
Aboon them a' ye tak your place
Painch, tripe or thairm:
Weel are ye wordy of a grace
As lang's my arm.

The groaning trencher there ye fill,
Your hurdies like a distant hill,
Your pin wad help to mend a mill
In time o' need,
While thro' your pores the dews distil
Like amber bread
His knife see rustic-labour dight,
An' cut you up wi' ready slight,
Trenching your gushing entrails bright,
Like onie ditch;
And then, O what a glorious sight,
Warm-reekin rich!

Then, horn for horn they stretch an' strive,
Deil tak the hindmost, on they drive,
Till a' their weel-swall'd kytes belyve
Are bent like drums;
Then auld Guidman, maist like to rive,
Bethankit hums.

Is there that owre his French ragout,
Or olio that wad staw a sow,
Or fricassee was mak her spew
Wi' perfect sconner,
Looks down wi' sneering, scornfu' view
On sic a dinner?

Poor devil! see him owre his trash,
As feckless as a withr'd rash,
His spindle shank a guid whip-lash,
His nieve a nit;
Thro' bluidy flood of field to dash,
O how unfit!

But mark the Rustic, haggis-fed,
The trembling earth resounds his tread,
Clap in his walie nieve a blade,
He'll mak it whissle;
An' legs, an' arms, an' heads will sned,
Like taps o' thrissle.

Ye Pow'rs wha mak mankind your care,
And dish them out their bill o' fare,
Auld Scotland wants nae skinking ware
That jaups in luggies;
But, if you wish her gratefu' pray'r,
Gie her a Haggis!

    At Burns Suppers we can also listen to works which reveal the more serious side to the poet's nature.
    Paper napkins often have the Selkirk Grace printed on them: —
    Some hae meat and canna eat,
    And some wad eat that want it,
    But we hae meat and we can eat,
    And sae the Lord be thanket.

FOR A' THAT

Is there, for honest poverty
That hangs his head, and a' that?
The coward-slave, we pass him by —
We dare poor for a' that!
For a' that, and a' that,
Our toils obscure and a' that,
The rank is but the guinea's stamp —
The man's the gowd for a' that.

What though on hamely fare we dine —
Wear hoddin grey, and a' that?
Gie fools their silks, and knaves their wine-
A man's a man for a' that:
For a' that and a' that,
Their tinsel show, and a' that;
The honest man, though e'er so poor,
Is king o' men for a' that.

Ye see yon birkie ca'd a lord,
Wha struts, and stares, and a' that;
Though hundreds worship at his word,
He's but a coof for a' that:
For a' that, and a' that:
His ribband, star, and a' that;
The man of independent mind,
He looks and laughs at a' that.

A prince can mak' a belted knight,
A marquis, duke, and a' that:
But an honest man's aboon his might,
Gude faith he mauna fa' that! (must not try that)
For a' that, and a' that,
Their dignities and a' that;
The pith o' sense, and pride o' worth,
Are higher rank than a' that.

Then let us pray that come it may,
As come it will for a' that,
That sense and worth, o'er a' the earth,
May bear the gree and a' that,

For a' that, and a' that,
It's comin yet for a' that,
That man to man, the warld o'er,
Shall brothers be for a' that!

Scotland the Brave

Hark when the night is falling,
Hear, hear the pipes are calling,
Loudly and proudly calling
Down through the glen.
There where the hills are sleeping,
Now feel the blood a-leaping,
High as the spirits of the old Highland men.

Towering in gallant fame,
Scotland, my mountain hame
High may your proud standards gloriously wave.
Land of the high endeavour,
Land of the shining river,
Land of my heart for ever,
Scotland the Brave.

High in the misty Highlands,
Out by the purple islands,
Brave are the hearts that beat
Beneath Scottish skies.

A RED, RED ROSE

O my Luve's like a red, red rose
   That's newly sprung in June.
O my Luve's like the melodie
   That's sweetly play'd in tune.

As fair art thou, my bonnie lass,
   So deep in luve am I;
And I will love thee still, my Dear,
   Till a' the seas gang dry.

Till a' the seas gang dry, my Dear,
  And the rocks melt wi' the sun:
I will love thee still, my Dear,
  While the sand o' life shall run:

And fare thee weel, my only Luve:
  and fare well, a while!
And I will come again, my Luve,
  Tho' it were ten thousand mile!

THE AULD WIFE'S LAMENT
(Or "Waley-waley for ma wallies")

As ah wis walkin' doon Woodfarm Road,
Ah heard an auld wife saying "Oh ma Goad"
An' as ah turned and went through the trees,
There she wis, doon oan her knees.

Says I tae her, "Aw, puir auld sowl,
Hae ye tummilt an' fell an' hurtit yersel?"
"Aw, naw," says she, "Ah wis daunerin' hame
Through Eastwood Park an' doon the wee lane.

Ah wis walkin' here an' walkin' there
Sniffin' awa' at the guid fresh air.
Ah bent doon tae look at a bonnie wee leaf,
An' ah opened ma mooth — an' loast ma teeth."

Well, we huntit East an' we huntit West,
At the hinner end we had tae rest,
An' the puir auld wife went hame a' begrutten,
Wi' no' a wally tae chow her mutton.

As ah walked oot the followin' morn,
Ah saw a magpie hameward gaun,
He fleed by me wi' a fearfu' grin —
The auld wife's teeth were stuck tae his chin!

BALACH BEAG NA DEISE GUIRME
(Little boy blue)

'Ille bhig na deise guirme,
Thig is seid an dudach;
An crodh air feadh an arbhair;
Sa' chluan tha na caoraich.
Ach cait a bheil an gille beag
Bu choir bhith toirt an aire orr'?
'Na shineadh ris an dig fheoir
Is srann aige 'na chadal!

Teagasg ga thoirt do mhnaoi bhuirb, mar bhuille ùird air iarunn fuar.
Chastising a termagant is like hammering cold iron.

A' CHAILLEACH SA' BHROIG
(The old woman who lived in a shoe)

An cual' thu mu'n chaillich
Bha fuireach sa' bhroig?
Bha 'n teaghlach cho lionmhor
Gun rian orr' no doigh.
Thug i dhaibh brochan
Gun aran, gun mharag;
Is sgailc i gu cruaidh iad
'Gan ruagadh do'n leabaidh.

MEILEAG! A CHAORA DHUBH
(Baa, baa, black sheep)

Meileag! A chaora dhubh,
Bheil cloimh agad an drasd'?
Tha, dhuin'-uasail, sin agam.
Tri poca lan—
Aon do'n mhaishistir,
Aon so bhean-an-taighe,
Is aon do'n a ghille bheag
Tha fuireach san t-sraid chuil.

GLAG AG GLAODHAICH
(Ding dong bell)

An glag ag glaodhaich cobhair
'S a' phiseach anns an tobar.
Co a chuir ann i ?
Co chuir ach Anndra!
Co a thug as i ?
Co thug ach Peadar!
Nach b'e sin am peasan crosd'
A dhol a bhathadh piseag bhochd
Nach do rinn de chron air thalamh
Ach sealg nan luch an sabhal athar!

Is minig a bha 'n donas daicheil.
The Devil is often attractive.

THE CLANSMAN'S TOAST

Whenever a social gathering or meeting of the Jacobite Clansman was being held, it was the duty of the Host to propose a Royal Toast, taking place after all guests had finished their meal. The host always sat at the head of the table while his wife or deputy sat at the other end. On a given signal, the host would have a punchbowl, **full of water,** placed in front of him. Rising with a charged glass in his hand, he would call his guests to order by declaring - "Ladies and Gentlemen, be so good as to have your glasses charged, for I will soon propose a toast."

It was usual for the ladies to ensure that everyone had a charged glass, and time being allowed for those having left the table to return to their rightful place. Rising for the second time, the host would rap the punch bowl three times with a spoon, thus drawing his guests to attention. "Ladies and Gentlemen, pray be upstanding for the Royal Toast!" The guests would then rise and on doing so, would hold their charged glasses in front of them. The host would then pass his glass over the punch bowl in a circular motion declaring — "Ladies and Gentlemen, a toast to our King o'er the water!" The Clansmen would immediately raise their glasses and on draining them, would ensure that their lips "kissed" the "Star", a sign of everlasting loyalty to the king o'er the water. Replying by shouting "AMEN", they would return their glasses to the table rapping the bottom of the glass twice on the table top, the sound representing the "Firing of Musketry" in defiance of the Union of 1707.

In modern times, the Clansman's Toast in no longer applicable to any cause but the tradition lives on in memory of those gallant Scots who were forced into emigration and/or exile to Canada, Australia, the United States and many other countries. Today we drop the "G" from "King" and the Royal Toast is presented to — "Our Kin O'er the Water and Auld Lang Syne".

"LORDS PRAYER"

AR N-ATHAIR a tha air neamh, Gu naomhaichear d'ainm. Thigeadh do rioghachd. Deanar do thoil air an talamh, mar a nithear air neamh. Tabhair dhuinn an diugh ar n-aran laitheil. Agus maith dhuinn ar fiachan, amhuil mar a mhaitheas sinne d'ar luchd-fiach. Agus na leig am buaireadh sinn. Ach saor sinn o'olc; oir is leatsa an rioghachd, agus a' ghloir, gu siorruidh.

Amen

Joseph R. Ross by Clan Ross tent.

JOSEPH R. ROSS.

The Author, born at Cape Negro, 1925, son of Captain William L. and Anna Jane Ross. Attended the Cape Negro School until his parents' death and then moved to Halifax, Montreal and Saskatoon where he completed his education. He spent more than 20 years as a medical worker with the Indians of Northern Manitoba and the Eskimos of the Arctic. In 1961 he was awarded the Federal Government Public Health award for writing health literature and was awarded the Medical Crest for life. After attending the University at Saskatoon he was Hospital Administrator for 18 years. In 1976 he was elected to a Fellowship in the Royal Society of Health, London, England. He is now retired spending the winters in England and summers at Blanche, Nova Scotia, which he calls home.

Acknowledgements — reference material.

The History Clan Ross — Alexander M. Ross.
Scotland. 1932.

The Highland Clearances — Lang Syne Publishers.
Scotland. 1986.

Tales of Highlands — Lang Syne Publishers.
Scotland, 1986

Kith and Kin of Scots — Lang Syne Publishers.
Scotland, 1986

Stories of the Clans — Lang Syne Publishers.
Scotland. 1986

The Earls of Ross — Francis Nevile Reid.
Scotland. 1894

The Highland Clearances — John Prebbles.
Scotland. 1963.

Tain Museum — Mrs. Mackenzie, Curator.
Scotland.

Public Records Office — Edinburgh, Scotland.

Public Library — Inverness, Scotland.

Private Material — Bonner Bridge, Scotland.

Balnagowan Castle — Mohamid Ali Fayer & Staff.

All Ross Ladies — that work in Tain Crowdie Cheese Factory.

Thank You.

www.ingramcontent.com/pod-product-compliance
Lightning Source LLC
Chambersburg PA
CBHW050642160426
43194CB00010B/1773